The Quilters' Cookbook

Simple Recipes for Busy Quilters

Cookbook Resources, LLC
Highland Village, Texas

The Quilters' Cookbook
Simple Recipes for Busy Quilters

Printed February 2011

International Standard Book Number: 978-1-59769-088-1

Library of Congress Control Number: 2010053809

Library of Congress Cataloging-in-Publication Data:

    The quilters' cookbook : simple recipes for busy quilters.
      p. cm.
    Includes index.
    ISBN 978-1-59769-088-1
    1. Quick and easy cooking. 2. Quilting. 3. Cookbooks. I. Cookbook Resources, LLC.
    TX833.5.Q58 2011
    641.5'55--dc22
                                     2010053809

Illustrations by Nancy Bohanan

Edited, Designed and Published in the United States of America
and Manufactured in China by

Cookbook Resources, LLC
541 Doubletree Drive
Highland Village, Texas 75077

Toll free 866-229-2665

www.cookbookresources.com

cookbook resources ® LLC
Bringing Family and Friends to the Table

The Quilters'

We want you to have more time for quilting and still have time to make home-cooked meals for your family, take a dip to a quilting party and make an easy casserole to take to the church supper.

Quick-and-easy recipes have 3 ingredients, 4 ingredients or 5 ingredients. The slow cooker recipes make it easy to prepare a meal in the morning, leave home and come back to a hot meal for the whole family. A special section of casseroles helps you make a dish when you need something fast and gifts in a jar make it fun to give special goodies.

You can do all this and be able to do one of the most important of duties: the family meal. The importance of family meals cannot be underestimated. The simple ritual of sitting down at the kitchen table and having a meal with moms and dads, brothers and sisters strengthens our homes and our country.

Harvard University's "Archives of Family Medicine" in March 2000 reported that families who ate together each week or almost every night had more nutrients and vitamins than those who did not eat together. Children got more calcium, iron, fiber, vitamin B6, vitamin C, vitamin E and ate less fat.

The University of Minnesota reported in their "The Archives of Pediatrics and Adolescent Medicine" in August 2004 that frequent family meals are directly related to better nutrition and to decreased risk of obesity and substance abuse.

When you have meals at home, you can teach children about good nutrition and social skills while helping create a home that feels nurturing and secure.

The meals don't have to be time-consuming; they can be very simple. The benefits from eating at home are amazing.

We hope this cookbook helps you to have simple meals and brings your family and friends to the table.

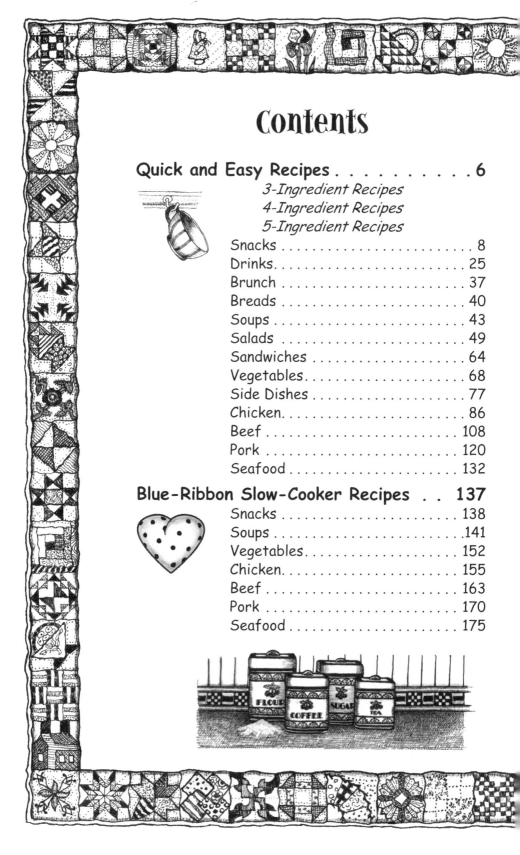

Contents

Contents

The history and evolution of quilting is interesting but elusive because it is not well documented. Quilting is centuries old and encompasses every culture, each of which has contributed to the advanced art status quilting enjoys today. It is believed that its humble beginnings arose out of necessity. Perhaps the first quilted items were undergarments worn for warmth.

It is an art form that has given thousands of women a creative outlet for their thoughts and talents and embraces warmth of home and friendship. Anyone who gives the special gift of a quilt can tell you it is stitched with love.

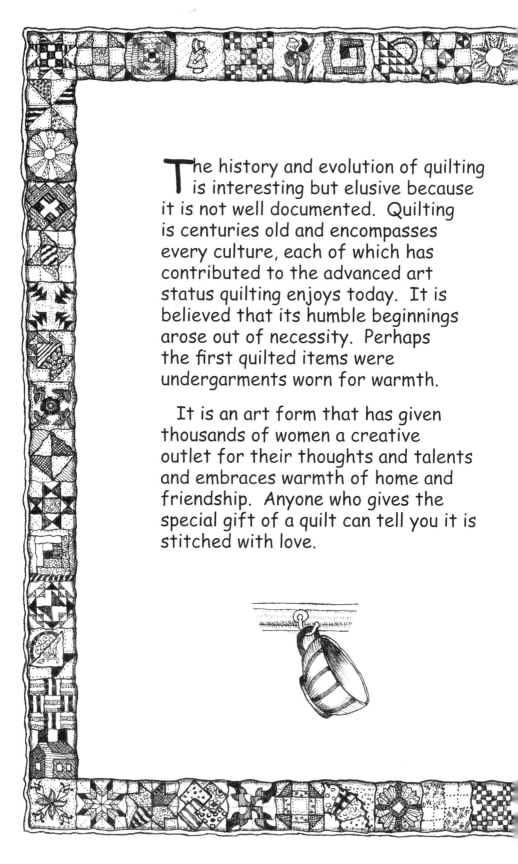

Quick and
Easy Recipes

Hot Creamy Artichoke Dip

1 (14 ounce) can artichoke hearts, drained, chopped
1 cup mayonnaise*
1 cup grated parmesan cheese
2 teaspoons prepared minced garlic

- Preheat oven to 350°. In bowl, combine all ingredients and mix well. Spoon mixture into sprayed 1½-quart glass baking dish.

- Bake uncovered for 25 minutes and serve with crackers or chips. Yields 2 cups.

TIP: This recipe has extended possibilities. For variety, add
   1 (6-ounce) can crabmeat or shrimp. Or try adding
   1 (10-ounce) package chopped spinach or ½ cup chopped,
   roasted red peppers.

*TIP: It is best not to use low-fat or lite mayonnaise.

Round-Up Veggie Dip

1 cup cottage cheese, drained
1 cup mayonnaise
1 (1 ounce) package ranch-style salad dressing mix

- In bowl, combine all ingredients and mix well.

- Refrigerate until ready to serve. Yields 1 cup.

No matter how hard you try, you can never baptize a cat.

Silly Dilly Dip

1 (8 ounce) carton sour cream
½ cup plain yogurt
1 bunch fresh green onions, tops only, chopped
2 teaspoons dried dill weed

- In bowl, combine sour cream, yogurt and a little salt and pepper. Fold in chopped onions and dried dill.

- Refrigerate several hours to blend flavors. Stir dip before serving. Serve with assortment of fresh vegetables. Yields 2 cups.

Creamy Olive Dip

1 (7 ounce) jar stuffed green olives, finely chopped
1 (8 ounce) package cream cheese, softened
½ cup chopped pecans

- Drain olives on paper towels.

- In mixing bowl, beat cream cheese until smooth. Combine olives and pecans into cream cheese mixture and mix well.

- Refrigerate before serving. Yields 1½ cups.

Cheesy Burger Dip

1 (32 ounce) package cubed Velveeta® cheese
1 (10 ounce) can diced tomatoes and green chilies
1 pound ground beef, browned, drained

- In saucepan over low heat, melt cheese with tomatoes and green chilies.

- Stir in meat and mix well. Heat thoroughly.

- Serve hot with large corn chips. Yields 3 cups.

Muy Bien Taco Dip

1 (8 ounce) package cream cheese, softened
1 (8 ounce) carton sour cream
1 (1 ounce) package taco seasoning mix

- In mixing bowl, beat cream cheese until smooth. Combine remaining ingredients and mix well. Cover and refrigerate until ready to serve.

- Serve with corn chips. Yields 1 cup.

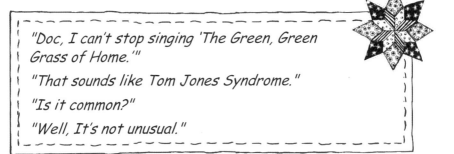

"Doc, I can't stop singing 'The Green, Green Grass of Home.'"

"That sounds like Tom Jones Syndrome."

"Is it common?"

"Well, It's not unusual."

Slow-Cook Pepe Gonzales Dip

1 pound pork sausage
2 (16 ounce) package cubed Velveeta® cheese
1 (10 ounce) can tomatoes and green chilies with liquid

- In skillet, brown sausage, crumble and drain well.

- Place all ingredients in slow cooker and heat thoroughly.

- Serve hot with tortilla chips. Yields 1 quart.

Chili-Cheese Tamale Dip

1 (15 ounce) can tamales
2 (15 ounce) cans chili
1 (8 ounce) package shredded cheddar cheese

- In bowl, mash tamales with fork and mix with chili.

- Place mixture in 9-inch glass pie plate and sprinkle cheddar cheese over top.

- Heat in 350° oven for 25 minutes or until bubbly.

- Serve with corn chips. Serves 10 to 12.

The earliest quilts preserved in the Smithsonian in Washington, D.C. date back to 1780.

Fiesta Break

1 (15 ounce) can tamales
1 (16 ounce) can chili without beans
1 cup salsa
2 (5 ounce) jars Old English cheese
1 cup finely chopped onion

- In bowl, mash tamales with fork.

- In saucepan, combine all ingredients and mix well. Heat thoroughly.

- Serve hot with crackers or chips. Serves 8 to 10.

Tasty Guacamole

3 avocados, peeled, seeded, mashed
1 cup thick and chunky salsa
$\frac{1}{2}$ cup cottage cheese, drained

- In bowl, combine all ingredients and $\frac{1}{4}$ teaspoon salt and mix well. Refrigerate.

- Serve as salad with Mexican food or as dip with tortilla chips. Serves 4

10 Good Reasons to Have Meals at Home are included in this cookbook. Here's one of them.

1. Family meals planned and prepared with the children's help will be more beneficial. It instills a sense of security, safety and nurturing that will be with children through their whole lives. When they help to plan and prepare meals, they are learning to be self-sufficient while building confidence to face the world on their own.

Festive Italian Dip

1 cup sun-dried tomato mayonnaise
½ cup sour cream
½ cup grated parmesan cheese
2 teaspoons dried basil
2 teaspoons minced garlic

• In bowl, combine all ingredients and mix well.

• Serve with vegetable sticks or breadsticks. Yields 2 cups.

Pizza Dippin' Dudes

1 large hamburger pizza, cooked
1 (26 ounce) jar chunky mushroom spaghetti sauce

• Cut pizza in half and then cut halves into 8 strips. Arrange on serving plate.

• In saucepan, heat spaghetti sauce and pour into round dish. Place dish in middle of serving plate with pizza strips. Serves 10.

TIP: To use this recipe for "supper", purchase your favorite pizza. There is a large selection of different-flavored spaghetti sauces. You can also buy a carton of refrigerated marinara sauce!

Colonial Williamsburg in Virginia is the world's largest living history museum. There are 500 restored and reconstructed historic buildings on 301 acres.

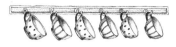

Ahoy Shrimp

1 (1 ounce) package dry onion soup mix
2 cups sour cream
1 cup chopped, cooked shrimp

- In mixing bowl, blend soup mix and 2 cups sour cream. Stir in shrimp.

- Cover and refrigerate for 2 hours before serving. Serve with crackers, chips, bread or veggies. Yields 3 cups.

Unbelievable Crab Dip

Absolutely delicious!

1 (16 ounce) package cubed Velveeta® cheese
2 (6½ ounce) cans crabmeat, drained
1 bunch fresh green onions with tops, chopped
2 cups mayonnaise
½ teaspoon seasoned salt

- Melt cheese in top of double boiler. Add remaining ingredients. Serve hot or at room temperature with wheat crackers. Serves 8 to 10.

TIP: *Don't count on your guests leaving the table until this dip is gone!*

---

10 Good Reasons to Have Meals at Home are included in this cookbook. Here's one of them.

2. Family meals offer quality time for all members of the family. It should be interactive with each family member sharing something about their day, their friends, their job, soccer practice, etc. Family meals provide stability and a sense of community that children need. By listening to adults, they increase their vocabulary, their social skills and their confidence.

Creamy Coconut Dip

1 (8 ounce) package cream cheese, softened
1 (15 ounce) can cream of coconut
1 (12 ounce) carton frozen whipped topping, thawed
1 teaspoon vanilla

• In large bowl, combine cream cheese and cream of coconut. Using mixer or wire whisk, blend until smooth. Fold in whipped topping and vanilla.

• Cover and refrigerate several hours before serving.

• Serve with graham crackers or fresh fruit. Serves 8 to 10.

Creamy Orange-Fruit Dip

1 (8 ounce) package cream cheese, softened
3 tablespoons orange juice concentrate
1 tablespoon orange zest
1 (7 ounce) jar marshmallow creme

• In mixing bowl, combine cream cheese, juice concentrate and orange zest. Mix well and fold in marshmallow crème. Cover and refrigerate.

• Serve with sliced apples, pears, strawberries and kiwifruit. Yields 2 cups.

It is not titles that honor men, but men who honor titles.

Lucy's Fresh Fruit Cream

1 (8 ounce) package cream cheese, softened
1 (7 ounce) jar marshmallow creme
¼ teaspoon ginger

• In mixing bowl, beat cream cheese until smooth.

• Combine remaining ingredients with cream cheese mixture and mix well.

• Serve with your favorite fresh fruits such as strawberries, banana slices and apple slices surrounding dip. Yields 2 cups.

Beef-Snack Spread

3 (8 ounce) packages cream cheese, softened
2 teaspoons lemon juice
¼ cup mayonnaise
½ teaspoon garlic powder
1 (5 ounce) jar dried beef, finely diced

• In bowl, combine all ingredients except dried beef and mix well. Fold in dried beef and combine with mixture.

• Refrigerate and serve on wheat crackers. Yields 2 cups.

10 Good Reasons to Have Meals at Home are included in this cookbook. Here's one of them.

3. Family meals are great for finding out about your children's lives. When children talk about their day and their activities, you learn what they are learning. You can explain important points and use these times as teaching moments. It is not a time for conflict or strong discipline, but a time for love and nurturing.

Zesty Chicken Spread

2 (12 ounce) cans white chicken, flaked, well drained
4 fresh green onions, finely chopped
1 (2 ounce) can diced pimento, drained
1 rib celery, finely chopped

Dressing:

1 (8 ounce) package cream cheese, softened
½ cup soup cream
1 tablespoon marinade for chicken
¼ teaspoon cayenne pepper

- In bowl, combine chicken, onions, pimento and celery and mix well.

- Using mixer, combine dressing ingredients plus generous amount of salt and mix well. Stir into chicken mixture and mix well. Refrigerate.

- Serve as a spread on butter crackers or wheat crackers. Serves 10.

Glazed Ham Snacks

⅓ cup chunky peanut butter
1 large slice cooked ham
⅓ cup packed brown sugar

- Spread peanut butter over ham slice and sprinkle brown sugar over top.

- Place ham under broiler 2 to 3 minutes or until peanut butter and sugar form brown crust.

- Place ham on cutting board and cut into 1-inch squares. Serve hot on wooden picks. Serves 6 to 8.

Ham and Cheese Pick-Ups

1 (8 ounce) package cream cheese, softened
1 (1 ounce) package dry onion soup mix
2 (3 ounce) packages thin sliced ham

- In mixing bowl, beat cream cheese until creamy and stir in soup mix. (Add a little mayonnaise or milk to make cream cheese easier to spread.)

- Lay slices of ham and spread thin layer of cream cheese mixture over each slice.

- Roll ham slices into log. Refrigerate for 1 to 2 hours.

- When ready to serve, slice into $\frac{3}{4}$-inch slices and lace wooden pick in each slice for easy pick-up. Serves 6.

Ham Pinwheels

9 thin slices, cooked ham
1 (5 ounce) jar olive-pimento spread
9 pickle sticks

- Spread olive-pimento mixture on thin slices of cooked ham.

- Lay pickle stick on ham and roll up. Slice or serve as pinwheels and secure with wooden picks. Serves 8 to 10.

Which runs faster... hot or cold?

Hot... everyone can catch cold.

Saucy Barbecued Sausages

This can be served from a slow cooker.

1 (18 ounce) bottle barbecue sauce
1 (12 ounce) jar grape jelly
2 (16 ounce) packages cocktail sausages

- Pour barbecue sauce and grape jelly into large saucepan.

- Cook and stir until jelly melts and mixture is smooth.

- Add cooked sausage and heat on low or simmer for 20 minutes. Stir often. Serve hot. Serves 8 to 10.

Sausage-Pineapple Bites

The "sweet and hot" makes a delicious combo.

1 pound link sausage, cooked, skinned
1 pound hot bulk sausage
1 (15 ounce) can crushed pineapple with juice
2 cups packed brown sugar
¼ teaspoon hot pepper sauce

- Slice link sausage into ⅓-inch pieces and shape bulk sausage into 1-inch balls. In skillet, brown sausage balls.

- In separate large saucepan, combine pineapple, brown sugar and hot pepper sauce. Heat thoroughly.

- Add both sausages and simmer for 30 minutes.

- Serve from chafing dish or small slow cooker with cocktail picks. Serves 10 to 12.

Sticky Chicky

30 chicken wings
½ cup honey
½ cup soy sauce

- Wash wings, cut into sections and discard tips.

- Pour honey and soy sauce into 9 x 13-inch pan and mix in pan. Arrange wings over mixture and refrigerate for 2 hours.

- Turn after 1 hour so both sides are "sticky". Bake in same pan at 375° for 45 minutes. Turn occasionally. Serves 10 to 15.

Calico Mushrooms

1 pound medium-size fresh mushrooms
1 (8 ounce) bottle Italian salad dressing
½ (8 ounce) package hot sausage, fried, crumbled
⅔ cup finely shredded mozzarella cheese

- Remove stems from mushrooms and brush with dressing. Place under broiler and broil for 5 minutes. Watch closely.

- Press sausage evenly into mushroom caps and sprinkle with cheese. Broil an additional 3 to 5 minutes. Serve hot. Serves 6 to 10.

The tradition of public dinners started in New England. A few of the most common include New England Boiled Dinner Suppers, Spaghetti Suppers, Meatloaf Suppers, Strawberry Suppers, Bean Suppers and Seafood Boils.

Olive Wraps

1 (12 ounce) can refrigerated buttermilk biscuits
1 (6 ounce) jar stuffed green olives
Grated parmesan cheese

- Cut each biscuit into quarters. Wrap dough around 1 olive.

- Roll in parmesan cheese and place on sprayed baking sheet.

- Bake at 350° for 6 to 8 minutes. Serves 8 to 10.

Nibbler's Nachos

1 pound lean ground beef
2 tablespoons chili powder
1 (15 ounce) can refried beans
1 (16 ounce) jar hot, chunky salsa
Tortilla chips

- In large skillet, brown ground beef and drain well. Add chili powder, refried beans, salsa and a little salt and mix well. Heat mixture until bubbly and stir constantly.

- Serve with tortilla chips on platter and spoon beef mixture over chips.

Topping:

1 (4 ounce) can chopped ripe olives
1 (8 ounce) package Mexican 4-cheese blend

- Sprinkle olives and cheese over beef mixture and serve immediately. Serves 8 to 10.

Hot Tuna Toast

2 (7 ounce) packages light tuna in water, drained
⅔ cup mayonnaise
½ cup shredded cheddar cheese
3 tablespoons chopped onion
3 tablespoons chopped celery
6 slices white or whole wheat bread

- In bowl, combine all ingredients except bread and mix well.

- Spread on white or whole wheat bread. Remove crusts.

- Cut each sandwich into 3 fingers and place on baking sheet.
  Toast under broiler and serve hot. Serves 6 to 8.

Gouda Cheese Wraps

1 (8 ounce) package crescent roll dough
1 (7 ounce) round gouda cheese, peeled
Butter, melted

- Shape dough into square. Wrap dough around peeled cheese
  round. Pinch edges together at top.

- Brush with melted butter and bake at 375° for about
  12 minutes.

- Set aside for 30 minutes before slicing. Slice in
  thin wedges. Serves 10 to 12.

A group of chess players were checking into a hotel and talked to each other in the lobby about a tournament. After some time, the hotel manager asked them to leave the lobby.

"Why?" said one of the players. "Because", he said, "I don't like a bunch of chess nuts boasting in an open foyer."

Walnut Finger Sandwiches

1 (8 ounce) package cream cheese, softened
½ cup mayonnaise
¾ cup finely chopped walnuts
½ cup finely chopped celery
Pumpernickel rye bread

- In mixing bowl, combine cream cheese and mayonnaise and blend well. Fold in walnuts and celery and mix well.

- Spread mixture on pumpernickel rye bread. Cut each sandwich in 3 strips. Yields about 2 cups spread.

Crunchy Munchies

1 (14 ounce) box cinnamon-swirl cereal
1 (9 ounce) can salted peanuts
1 (9 ounce) can whole cashews
1 cup (2 sticks) butter
1½ cups packed brown sugar

- In large bowl, combine cereal, peanuts and cashews. In saucepan, combine butter and brown sugar and heat until sugar dissolves. Remove from heat and pour butter-sugar mixture over cereal and nuts. Stir and coat well.

- Spread mixture evenly on 2 sprayed baking sheets. Set aside to cool.

- Break apart when ready to serve. Yields 1 quart.

Microwave Buttered Walnuts

1 pound walnut halves
1 teaspoon seasoned salt
¼ cup (½ stick) butter

• Place walnuts in 1½-quart microwave-safe dish. Add salt and dot with butter.

• Microwave on HIGH for 1 to 2 minutes. Stir until butter coats nuts evenly. Yields 2 cups.

Spanish Peanut-Coconut Clusters

6 (2 ounce) squares white chocolate coating, chopped
1 (12 ounce) package milk chocolate chips
½ cup flaked coconut
1 (12 ounce) can Spanish peanuts

• In heavy saucepan over low heat, melt white and milk chocolate. Stir constantly. Remove from heat and stir in coconut and peanuts.

• Drop by tablespoons on baking sheet lined with wax paper. Refrigerate. Serves about 8 to 10.

The first recipe for pancakes or "slapjacks" was recorded in America's first cookbook, American Cookery, *in 1796. They were made with pumpkin puree, cornmeal and egg. They were fried on a griddle and served with maple syrup.*

Sunny Orchard Punch

1 (46 ounce) can apricot juice, chilled
1 (2 liter) bottle ginger ale, chilled
½ gallon orange sherbet

- When ready to serve, combine juice and ginger ale in punch bowl.

- Stir in scoops of orange sherbet. Serve in 4-ounce cups punch.

- Yields about 36 cups punch.

Cranberry-Grape Frost

1 (48 ounce) bottle cranberry juice, chilled
1 (46 ounce) can grape juice, chilled
½ gallon raspberry sherbet

- Combine cranberry and grape juices in punch bowl.

- Add scoops of raspberry sherbet and mix well. Yields about 36 cups punch.

TIP: Add 1 (2 liter) bottle chilled ginger ale or 7UP®. if you want to add something bubbly.

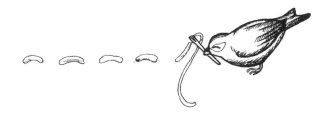

Cranberry Fizzle

2 quarts cranberry juice, chilled
2 quarts ginger ale or 7UP®, chilled
1 (12 ounce) can frozen lemonade concentrate

• Combine all ingredients in punch bowl and mix well.

• Add 2 cans ice water. Yields about 24 cups punch.

Cranberry Splash

1 (2 liter) bottle lemon-lime carbonated drink, chilled
1 (2 quart) bottle cranberry juice, chilled
1 (2 quart) bottle apple juice, chilled
1 (64 ounce) bottle sparkling grape juice, chilled

• In punch bowl, combine all ingredients.

• Serve over ice. Yields about 36 cups punch.

Maine is responsible for 90% of the U.S. lobster supply and for about 25% of all blueberries grown in North America. More wild blueberries grow in Maine than any other place in the world.

Ginger Ale Fruit Punch

1 (48 ounce) bottle cranberry juice drink
1 (48 ounce) can pineapple juice
½ cup sugar
2 teaspoons almond extract
1 (2 liter) bottle ginger ale, chilled

- In bowl, combine juices, sugar and almond extract. Stir until sugar dissolves.

- Cover and refrigerate 8 hours.

- When ready to serve, add ginger ale and stir. Yields about 36 cups punch.

Cranberry-Sherbet Slurpy

½ gallon cranberry juice, chilled
1 quart ginger ale, chilled
½ gallon pineapple sherbet

- Combine juice and ginger ale in punch bowl.

- Stir in sherbet before serving. Yields about 16 cups punch.

An excellent health tip:
Forgive Everyone for Everything.

Orange-Cranberry Cocktail

3 cups cranberry juice, chilled
1 cup sugar
1 (6 ounce) can frozen orange juice concentrate, thawed
3 (12 ounce) cans club soda, chilled

- In large pitcher, combine cranberry juice, sugar and orange juice concentrate. Stir well until sugar dissolves. Cover and refrigerate for 1 hour.

- When ready to serve, stir in chilled club soda. Serve cocktail over crushed ice. Serves 20 to 24.

Fizzy Strawberry Cooler

1 (6 ounce) can frozen limeade concentrate
1 (10 ounce) package frozen strawberries, thawed
1 (2 liter) bottle strawberry carbonated beverage, chilled

- Prepare limeade according to directions on can. Refrigerate.

- Blend berries in blender until smooth.

- Combine limeade and berries.

- When ready to serve, stir in strawberry carbonated beverage. Serves about 20.

By the time we learn the rules of life, we're too old to play the game.

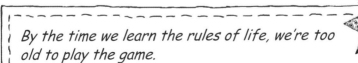

Strawberry Slush

2 (10 ounce) boxes frozen strawberries, thawed
1 (12 ounce) can frozen pink lemonade concentrate
1 (2 liter) bottle 7UP® or ginger ale, chilled

* In blender, mix berries until slushy.

* Prepare lemonade according to directions on can. Refrigerate.

* Pour lemonade into punch bowl and stir in berries. Add 7UP® or ginger ale and mix well. Yields 20 to 24 cups punch.

TIP: If this punch is too tart, add ½ cup sugar.

Strawberry-Spritzer Punch

3 (10 ounce) packages frozen strawberries, thawed, divided
2 (24 ounce) bottles white grape juice, chilled
1 (28 ounce) bottle club soda, chilled

* In blender, place 2 packages thawed strawberries with juice and blend until smooth.

* In punch bowl, combine blended berries, grape juice and remaining package of strawberries. Mix well.

* When ready to serve, stir in club soda. Yields 20 to 24 cups punch.

We are all time travelers moving at the speed of exactly 60 seconds per minute or 3,600 seconds per hour.

Five Alive Glory

2 (12 ounce) cans frozen Five Alive® juice concentrate
1 (12 ounce) can frozen pink lemonade concentrate
1 (2 liter) bottle ginger ale, chilled

- Dilute juices according to can directions and mix in punch bowl.

- When ready to serve, add ginger ale. Yields about 36 cups punch.

Spritely Punch

2 (2 liter) bottles Sprite®, chilled
1 (46 ounce) plus 3 (6 ounce) cans pineapple juice, chilled
1 gallon orange sherbet

- Combine Sprite® and pineapple juice in punch bowl.

- Spoon in sherbet and mix well. Serves about 24 to 28.

When you wake up alive in the morning, thank God for it.

Hoola Dance Cooler

1 (46 ounce) can Hawaiian Punch, chilled
1 (2 liter) bottle ginger ale or 7UP®, chilled
1 (12 ounce) can frozen lemonade concentrate

• Combine ingredients in punch bowl. Mix in 2 cups cold water.

• Serve immediately. Yields about 36 cups punch.

Party Fruit Punch

2 quarts cranberry juice, chilled, divided
1 (46 ounce) can fruit punch, chilled
1 (46 ounce) can pineapple juice, chilled

• Pour 1-quart cranberry juice into ice trays and freeze as ice cubes.

• In punch bowl, combine fruit punch, pineapple juice and remaining 1-quart cranberry juice and mix well.

• When ready to serve, add cranberry ice cubes. Yields about 36 cups punch.

No matter how old a mother is, she watches her middle-aged children for signs of improvement.
-Florida Scott-Maxwell

Pineapple-Slush Punch

1 (46 ounce) can pineapple juice, chilled
1 (46 ounce) can apple juice, chilled
2 (28 ounce) bottles 7UP®, chilled

- Freeze pineapple and apple juices in their cans. Set out juices to thaw about 1 hour before serving.

- When ready to serve, combine all ingredients in punch bowl. Yields about 36 cups punch.

Cappuccino Punch

This is so good you will want a big glass of it!

1 gallon strong, brewed coffee
½ cup sugar
3 tablespoons vanilla
2 (16 ounce) cartons half-and-half cream
1 gallon vanilla ice cream, softened

- Combine sugar with coffee and refrigerate. (Add more sugar if you prefer it sweeter.)

- Add vanilla and half-and-half to mixture.

- When ready to serve, add ice cream to mixture in punch bowl. Yields about 24 cups punch.

Life is too short to waste energy hating someone. Don't hate anyone.

Mocha Punch

1 quart coffee, chilled
1 quart chocolate milk
1 quart vanilla or chocolate ice cream

- Mix coffee and milk until they blend well.

- Just before serving, stir in ice cream and mix until creamy. Serves about 10 to 12.

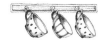

Anniversary Punch

1 (2 quart) bottle white grape juice, chilled
1 (46 ounce) bottle pineapple juice, chilled
½ gallon vanilla ice cream
2 quarts ginger ale, chilled

- In punch bowl, combine juices and stir.

- Add scoops of ice cream and pour in ginger ale. Stir lightly and serve. Serves 24 to 30.

Why couldn't the sesame seed leave the casino?

Because he was on a roll.

Holiday Party Blend

1 (750 milliliter) bottle dry white wine, chilled
1 (750 milliliter) bottle champagne, chilled
½ cup frozen orange juice concentrate, thawed
⅓ cup frozen lemonade concentrate, thawed

• Combine all ingredients in large pitcher.

• Serve over chipped ice. Serves about 20 to 24.

Christmas Punch

1 (46 ounce) can pineapple juice, chilled
1 (1 liter) bottle ginger ale, chilled
1 (2 liter) bottle strawberry-carbonated beverage, chilled

• Combine all ingredients in punch bowl.

• Use extra ginger ale or 7UP®, if desired. Serves about 20.

Virgin Champagne Punch

2 (32 ounce) bottles white grape juice, chilled, divided
2 (25 ounce) bottles sparkling white grape juice, chilled
2 (2 liter) bottles ginger ale, chilled
1 (6 ounce) can frozen lemonade concentrate, thawed, undiluted

- Use 1 bottle white grape juice to make ice ring. Keep frozen until ready to serve.

- When ready to serve, combine all remaining ingredients in large punch bowl and add ice ring. Yields 36 cups punch.

TIP: *Use a round gelatin mold with a hole in the center for the ice ring.*

Homemade Amaretto

3 cups sugar
1 pint vodka
3 tablespoons almond extract
1 tablespoon vanilla (not imitation)

- In large pan, combine sugar and $2\frac{1}{4}$ cups water and heat until it boils.

- Reduce heat and simmer 5 minutes. Stir occasionally.

- Remove from stove. Add vodka, almond extract and vanilla and mix well.

- Store in airtight jar. Yields 2 pints.

I am not young enough to know everything.
-Oscar Wilde

Homemade Kahlua

3 cups hot water
1 cup instant coffee granules
4 cups sugar
1 quart vodka
1 vanilla bean, split

- In large saucepan, combine hot water, coffee granules and sugar and mix well.

- Boil for 2 minutes and cool.

- Add vodka and vanilla bean to mixture and pour into bottle or jar.

- Set aside for 30 days before serving. Shake occasionally. Yields 2 quarts.

TIP: If you have Mexican vanilla, make "instant" kahlua by substituting 3 tablespoons Mexican vanilla instead of 1 vanilla bean. You won't have to wait 30 days.

Kahlua Frosty

1 cup Kahlua® liqueur
1 pint vanilla ice cream
1 (8 ounce) carton half-and-half cream
$\frac{1}{8}$ teaspoon almond extract
$1\frac{2}{3}$ cups crushed ice

- In blender, combine all ingredients and process until smooth.

- Serve immediately. Serves 6 to 8.

Buttons 'n Bows Breakfast Bake

*This is a favorite for overnight guests and
special enough for Christmas morning.*

1 pound hot sausage, cooked, crumbled
1 cup shredded cheddar cheese
1 cup biscuit mix
5 eggs, slightly beaten
2 cups milk

- Place cooked and crumbled sausage in sprayed 9 x 13-inch baking dish and sprinkle with cheese.

- In mixing bowl, combine biscuit mix, eggs and a little salt. Beat well. Add milk and stir until fairly smooth. Pour over sausage mixture.

- Bake at 350° for 35 minutes. (You can prepare mixture night before cooking and refrigerate.) To cook following morning, add 5 minutes to cooking time. Serves 4.   38

Green Chile Squares

2 (4 ounce) cans diced green chilies
1 (8 ounce) package shredded sharp cheddar cheese
8 eggs, beaten
½ cup half-and-half cream

- Place green chilies in 9 x 13-inch baking dish and cover with cheese.

- In bowl, combine remaining ingredients with a little salt and pepper and mix well.

- Pour mixture over chilies and cheese and bake at 350° for 30 minutes.

- Set aside at room temperature for few minutes before cutting into squares. Serves about 8.

Pineapple-Cheese Casserole

This is really a different recipe and so good.

2 (20 ounce) cans unsweetened pineapple chunks, drained
1 cup sugar
5 tablespoons flour
1½ cups shredded cheddar cheese
1 stack Town House® or Ritz® crackers, crushed
½ cup (1 stick) butter, melted

• Spray 9 x 13-inch baking dish and layer ingredients in
  following order: pineapple, sugar-flour mixture, shredded
  cheese and cracker crumbs.

• Drizzle butter over casserole and bake at 350° for
  25 minutes or until bubbly. Serves about 8 to 10.

TIP: This can be served for brunch or lunch.

Cloverleaf Rolls

2¼ cups biscuit mix, divided
1 (8 ounce) carton sour cream
½ cup (1 stick) butter, melted

• In bowl, combine 2 cups biscuit mix, sour cream and melted
  butter and mix well.

• Sprinkle remaining ¼ cup biscuit mix on sheet of wax paper.

• Drop dough by level tablespoonfuls onto biscuit mix and roll
  into balls.

• Place 3 balls into each of 12 sprayed muffin cups and bake
  at 350° for 15 to 20 minutes or until golden brown. Yields 12.

French Onion Biscuits

2 cups biscuit mix
¼ cup milk
1 (8 ounce) carton French onion dip

• In bowl, combine all ingredients and mix until soft dough forms. Drop dough into mounds onto sprayed baking sheet.

• Bake at 375° for 10 to 12 minutes or until golden brown. Serves 8 to 10.

TIP: If you like round, cut-out biscuits, sprinkle extra biscuit mix on wax paper and spoon dough over biscuit mix. Sprinkle about 1 tablespoon biscuit mix over dough and knead 3 or 4 times. Use a little more biscuit mix if dough is too sticky. Pat out to ½-inch thickness and cut with biscuit cutter.

Hot Cheesy Bread Slices

1 (8 ounce) package shredded cheddar cheese
1 cup mayonnaise
1 loaf French bread, cut in ½-inch slices

• In bowl, combine cheese and mayonnaise and mix well.

• Spread on bread slices and place on baking sheet.

• Bake at 350° for 8 to 10 minutes. Serves 8.

TIP: For variety, mix 2 cheeses (cheddar and Swiss) with mayonnaise and spread on bread.

Nine out of ten tomatoes in the U.S. are grown in California. Over 85% of home gardeners grow tomatoes.

Chile Bread

1 loaf Italian bread, unsliced
½ cup (1 stick) butter, melted
1 (4 ounce) can diced green chilies, drained
¾ cup shredded Monterey Jack cheese

- Slice bread almost all the way through.

- Combine butter, chilies and cheese and mix well. Spread between bread slices.

- Cover loaf with foil and bake at 350° for 15 minutes.

Mexican Cornbread

1 (8 ounce) box Mexican Velveeta® cheese, cubed
¾ cup milk
2 (8 ounce) packages corn muffin mix
2 eggs, beaten

- Preheat oven to 375°.

- Melt cheese with milk in saucepan over low heat and stir constantly. Combine corn muffin mix and eggs in bowl. Fold in cheese and mix just until moist.

- Pour into sprayed, floured 9 x 13-inch baking pan.

- Bake for about 25 minutes or until light brown. Yields 12 to 16 squares.

French fries refer to the French way of deep frying potatoes in oil. In 1802, Thomas Jefferson had "potatoes served in the French way" as well as macaroni and cheese for a White House dinner while President of the United States.

No-Peek Popovers

2 eggs
1 cup milk
1 cup flour

- In bowl, combine all ingredients and mix well. Fill 8 sprayed muffin cups three-fourths full.

- Place in cold oven, bake at 450° for 30 minutes and don't peek. Serves 6.

Crunchy Breadsticks

Keep these made up in the freezer. Everyone loves them and no one will believe they are hot dog buns!

1 package hot dog buns
1 cup (2 sticks) butter, melted
Garlic powder
Paprika

- Take each bun half and slice in half lengthwise. Using pastry brush, spread butter over breadsticks.

- Sprinkle with a little garlic powder and paprika.

- Place on baking sheet and bake at 225° for 45 minutes. Serves 8.

*Don't walk in front of me, I may not follow.
Don't walk behind me, I may not lead. Just walk beside me and be my friend.*
                    -Unknown

Quick Zucchini Bread

1 (18 ounce) box spice cake mix
2 cups shredded zucchini
½ cup chopped black walnuts or pecans

• Prepare cake mix according to package directions.

• Squeeze liquid from zucchini. Stir zucchini and nuts into cake mix and mix well.

• Pour into 2 greased, floured loaf pans and bake at 350° for 50 to 60 minutes. Serves 8 to 16.

Most block patterns have several different names depending upon the region they reflect. Patterns were named for customs, news-making events, life experiences and beliefs. Here are a few examples.

Biblical:
"Joseph's Coat"
"Cross and Crown"
"David and Goliath"
"Star of Bethlehem"
"Jacobs Ladder"

Nature:
"Grandmother's Flower Garden"
"Spider Web"
"Autumn Leaf"
"Delectable Mountain"
"Sunflower"
"Clamshell"

Political:
"Liberty Star"
"Spirit of St. Louis"
"White House Steps"
"Fifty-Forty or Fight"
"President's Wreath"

Pioneer:
"Log Cabin"
"Rail Fence"
"Broken Wheel"
"Mohawk"
"Churn Dash"

Wild Broccoli-Rice Soup

This is a hardy and delicious soup – full of flavor.

1 (6 ounce) package chicken-flavored wild rice mix
1 (10 ounce) package frozen chopped broccoli, thawed
2 teaspoons dried minced onion
1 (10 ounce) can cream of chicken soup
1 (8 ounce) package cream cheese, cubed

- In large saucepan, combine rice, seasoning packet and
  6 cups water.

- Bring to boil and reduce heat. Cover and simmer for
  10 minutes. Stir once.

- Add broccoli and onion and simmer another 5 minutes. Stir
  in soup and cream cheese. Cook and stir until cheese melts.
  Serves about 4 to 6.

Cozy Chicken-Noodle Soup

This great for leftover chicken or turkey.

3 (15 ounce) cans chicken broth
1 (15 ounce) can sliced carrots, drained
1 cup sliced celery
$\frac{2}{3}$ cup uncooked medium egg noodles
2 cups diced, cooked chicken or turkey

- In large saucepan, combine all ingredients. Bring to boil.

- Reduce heat and simmer for 15 minutes or until noodles
  are done. Serves 6 to 8.

A friend is a gift you give yourself.
-Robert Lewis Stevenson

Creamy Tomato Soup

2 (10 ounce) cans tomato soup
2 (15 ounce) cans Mexican stewed tomatoes
1 (10 ounce) can chicken broth
1 (8 ounce) carton sour cream

• In large saucepan, combine tomato soup, stewed tomatoes, broth and 1 soup can water. Bring to boil, reduce heat and simmer for 10 minutes.

• Serve with sour cream dollop on top of each soup bowl. Serves about 6.

Snappy Tomato Soup

1 (10 ounce) can tomato soup
1 (14 ounce) can chopped stewed tomatoes with onion
1 (10 ounce) can chopped tomatoes and green chilies

• In saucepan, mix all ingredients plus 1 soup can water.

• Heat to boiling and stir often.

• Reduce heat and simmer for 5 minutes. Serves about 4.

An excellent health tip: Play More Games.

Tasty French Onion-Tomato Soup

2 (10 ounce) cans tomato bisque soup
1 (15 ounce) can stewed tomatoes
2 (10 ounce) cans French onion soup
1 (14 ounce) can chicken broth

- In large saucepan, combine all ingredients plus 2 soup cans water.

- Bring to boil, reduce heat and simmer for 15 minutes. Serves about 6 to 8.

Harvest Potato Soup

2 (14 ounce) cans chicken broth seasoned with garlic
2 large potatoes, peeled, cubed
1 onion, finely chopped
1 (4 ounce) package cooked, crumbled real bacon, divided

- In saucepan, combine broth, 1 cup water, potatoes, onion and ½ bacon and heat to boil. Reduce heat and cook on medium for 25 minutes.

- Sprinkle remaining bacon bits on individual servings. Serves 4.

In 1782, the American bald eagle was selected as the national emblem of the United States. Eagles were prominently displayed in quilts for the remaining 1700's.

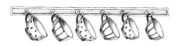

Mama's Favorite Ham-Bean Soup

1 cup chopped celery
1 cup chopped onion
3 (15 ounce) cans navy beans with liquid
2 (15 ounce) cans chicken broth
2 - 3 cups cooked ham, cubed
1 teaspoon chili powder

- In large saucepan with a little oil, saute celery and onion. Add remaining ingredients and bring to boil. Reduce heat and cook for 15 minutes. Serves 4 to 6.

TIP: For more color, add sliced carrots.

Pop's Navy Bean Soup

3 (14 ounce) cans navy beans with liquid
1 (14 ounce) can chicken broth
1 cup chopped ham
1 large onion, chopped
½ teaspoon garlic powder

- In large saucepan, combine beans, broth, ham, onion and garlic powder.

- Add 1 cup water and bring to boil. Simmer until onion is tender crisp.

- Serve hot with cornbread. Serves 4.

Quick All-Seasons Vegetable Soup

1 (19 ounce) can minestrone soup
1 (16 ounce) package frozen mixed vegetables
1 (15 ounce) can seasoned pinto beans
1 (15 ounce) can Italian stewed tomatoes

- In large saucepan, combine all ingredients and heat to boil.

- Reduce heat and simmer for 15 minutes. Serves 6.

Thanksgiving Soup

1 (10 ounce) can cream of chicken soup
1 (10 ounce) can cream of celery soup
2 (14 ounce) cans chicken broth
1 (16 ounce) package frozen mixed vegetables
1 (12 ounce) can turkey or leftover turkey

- In large saucepan, combine all ingredients. Bring to boil.

- Reduce heat to medium and cook for 15 minutes. Serves 6 to 8.

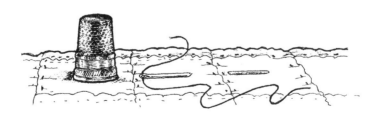

Quick Beef Stew

1 pound boneless, beef sirloin steak, cut into 1-inch cubes
1 (10 ounce) can tomato soup
1 (10 ounce) can French onion soup
1 (15 ounce) can Mexican stewed tomatoes
1 (16 ounce) package frozen mixed vegetables

- In soup pot with a little oil, brown steak cubes. Lower heat and simmer 5 minutes. Stir several times. Add soups, stewed tomatoes, mixed vegetables and ½ cup water.

- Cover and cook over low-to-medium heat for 10 minutes or until vegetables are tender. Serves 6 to 8.

Snuggle-Up Roast Beef Stew

2 cups cubed leftover roast
1 (10 ounce) can French onion soup
1 (10 ounce) can beef broth
1 (1 ounce) package brown gravy mix
1 (15 ounce) can cubed potatoes
1 (15 ounce) can cut green beans

- In roasting pan, combine all ingredients plus 2 cups water. Bring to boil, reduce heat and simmer for 20 to 25 minutes.

- Serve with cornbread or crackers. Serves 4 to 6.

Education's purpose is to replace an empty mind with an open one.
              -Malcolm Forbes

Patchwork Broccoli-Waldorf Salad

6 cups fresh broccoli florets
1 large red apple with peel, chopped
½ cup golden raisins
½ cup chopped pecans
½ cup prepared coleslaw dressing

• In large bowl, combine broccoli, apple, raisins and pecans.

• Drizzle salad mixture with dressing and toss to coat.
  Refrigerate before serving. Serves 6 to 8.

Broccoli-Green Bean Salad

1 large bunch broccoli, cut into florets
2 (15 ounce) cans cut green beans, drained
1 bunch fresh green onions with tops, chopped
2 (6 ounce) jars marinated artichoke hearts, chopped, drained
1½ cups original ranch salad dressing with mayonnaise

• Combine broccoli, green beans, onions and artichokes and
  mix well.

• Add dressing and toss.

• Refrigerate for 24 hours before serving. Serves 6 to 8.

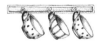

*Eat more foods grown on plants than those
manufactured in plants.*

Broccoli-Mushroom Salad

1 large bunch broccoli cut into florets
1 (16 ounce) carton fresh mushrooms, stemmed
1 bunch fresh green onions, cut into 1-inch slices
½ (8 ounce) bottle Italian salad dressing

- In salad bowl, combine broccoli, mushrooms and green onions.

- Toss with dressing and refrigerate. Serves 6 to 8.

Crazy Quilter's Nutty Slaw

2 (3 ounce) packages chicken-flavored ramen noodles
1 (16 ounce) package broccoli slaw
1 cup slivered almonds, toasted
1 cup sunflower seeds, toasted
1 (8 ounce) bottle Italian salad dressing

- In large bowl, combine broken noodles, broccoli slaw, almonds and sunflower seeds.

- Sprinkle ramen noodle seasoning packets over salad and toss with dressing. Refrigerate several hours Serves 10 to 12.

TIP: To toast almonds and sunflower seeds, place in 275° oven for 10 to 15 minutes.

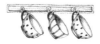

Spend time with people over 70 and under the age of 6.

Crunchy Chicken Salad Supper

1 (8 ounce) package coleslaw mix
2 cups fresh small broccoli florets
$\frac{1}{3}$ cup salted roasted peanuts
$\frac{1}{3}$ cup sesame seeds, toasted
$\frac{2}{3}$ - $\frac{3}{4}$ cup creamy dijon-style mayonnaise
1 - 2 cups leftover cooked chicken strips

• In bowl, combine coleslaw mix, broccoli and black pepper.
  Sprinkle in peanuts and sesame seeds with enough dijon-style
  mayonnaise to hold mixture together.

• Place on individual serving plates with strips of chicken strips
  over top. Serves 4 to 6.

Crunchy Carrot Salad

1 (16 ounce) package shredded carrots
1 cup golden raisins
$\frac{3}{4}$ cup chopped cashews
$\frac{1}{2}$ - $\frac{2}{3}$ cup mayonnaise

• In bowl, combine carrots, raisins and cashews and mix.

• Add ample amount mayonnaise to mixture so that it is
  not dry. Serves 6 to 8.

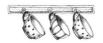

*Middle age is when you've met so many people
that every new person you meet reminds you of
someone else.*
        -Ogden Nash

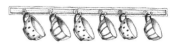

Sweet Orange Coleslaw

3 cups coleslaw mix
2 cups cooked brown rice
2 tart green apples with peel, finely chopped
½ cup chopped pecans, toasted

Dressing:

½ cup frozen orange juice concentrate
½ cup mayonnaise
½ teaspoon dijon-style mustard
½ teaspoon seasoned salt

- In salad bowl, combine coleslaw mix, rice and apples. In separate bowl, combine all dressing ingredients and mix well.

- Toss dressing with slaw-apple mixture. Stir in pecans. Refrigerate. Serves 8 to 10.

TIP: Toast pecans at 275° for 10 minutes.

Cucumbers with Bow Ties

1 (8 ounce) package bow-tie pasta, cooked, drained
1 (16 ounce) package frozen green peas, thawed
½ seedless cucumber, halved, sliced
1 small red onion, sliced
1 (16 ounce) jar ranch-style salad dressing, chilled

- In large bowl, combine cooked pasta, peas, cucumber slices, onion and a little salt.

- Toss with about ½ cup salad dressing (or more if desired). Serves 6 to 8.

Courthouse Steps Layered Salad

1 (10 ounce) package mixed salad greens
1 seedless cucumber, peeled, coarsely chopped
1 (10 ounce) package frozen green peas, thawed, drained
1 red bell pepper, chopped

Topping:

¾ cup chunky bleu cheese salad dressing
1 (4 ounce) package crumbled real bacon
1 cup shredded mozzarella cheese

- In salad bowl with 4-inch sides, layer all ingredients. Mix with bleu cheese dressing and sprinkle bacon and cheese over top of salad. Refrigerate. Serves 8.

TIP: *The seedless cucumbers are so much better than the regular cucumbers! Ranch salad dressing is a good substitute if you don't like bleu cheese.*

Marinated Cucumbers

3 cucumbers, thinly sliced
2 (4 ounce) jars chopped pimentos, drained
⅔ cup oil
¼ cup white wine vinegar
1 (8 ounce) carton sour cream

- Combine cucumber and pimentos. Mix in oil, vinegar and ½ teaspoon salt.

- Pour over cucumbers and refrigerate for 1 hour.

- To serve, drain well and pour sour cream over cucumbers and pimentos. Serves 8 to 12.

Salad Toss for a Gathering

1 (16 ounce) package multi-colored spiral pasta
1 bunch broccoli, cut into florets
1 bunch cauliflower, cut into florets
1 red bell pepper, julienned
1 (10 ounce) package frozen peas, thawed
1 (8 ounce) chunk mozzarella cheese, cubed
1 (16 ounce) bottle creamy Italian salad dressing

- Cook pasta according to package directions, drain and rinse in cold water. Stir in broccoli, cauliflower, bell pepper, peas and cheese. Mix well.

- Toss with dressing. Cover and refrigerate several hours before serving. Serves 12 to 14.

Southwest Retreat Salad

1 (10 ounce) package mixed salad greens
1 (15 ounce) can whole kernel corn, drained
1 (15 ounce) can black beans, drained
2 tomatoes, chopped, well drained
½ cup ranch-style salad dressing
½ cup chunky salsa

Topping:

1 (8 ounce) package shredded Mexican 4-cheese blend
2½ cups broken tortilla chips

- Place salad greens in large salad bowl with 4 to 5-inch sides. Layer corn, back beans and tomatoes. Combine dressing and salsa and spoon over salad.

- Sprinkle cheese and tortilla chips over top of salad and serve immediately. Serves about 8 to 10.

Fruity Blueberry Salad

2 (3 ounce) boxes grape gelatin
1 (20 ounce) can blueberry pie filling
1 (20 ounce) can crushed pineapple with liquid

- Dissolve gelatin using 1 cup boiling water.

- Refrigerate until partially set and stir in blueberries and pineapple with liquid.

- Pour into 9 x 13-inch glass dish and refrigerate until firm. Serves 12.

Cranberry-Orange Relish

1 (16 ounce) can whole berry cranberries
⅓ cup orange marmalade
⅓ cup chopped walnuts

- Combine all ingredients and mix well.

- Cover and refrigerate 2 to 3 hours before serving.

- Serve with pork or ham. Serves 6 to 8.

TIP: You may substitute ½ cup sliced maraschino cherries for walnuts.

10 Good Reasons to Have Meals at Home are included in this cookbook. Here's one of them.

4. Family meals help children learn the basics of good nutrition and how to take care of themselves. Family meals don't have to be big deals, but can be simple meals with basic nutrition. Children learn how to strive for good health and how they are responsible for themselves. Family meals provide a time for family traditions and family memories to grow.

Sunshine Berry Salad

1½ cups apple cider
1 (6 ounce) package orange gelatin
1 (16 ounce) can whole cranberry sauce
1 (8 ounce) can crushed pineapple with liquid

• In saucepan, boil 1 cup cider. Pour over gelatin and mix until gelatin dissolves. Stir in remaining apple cider, whole cranberry sauce and pineapple. Mix well.

• Pour into 9-inch ring mold and refrigerate. Use knife around edges of mold to remove before serving. Place on serving plate and fill center with fresh fruit. Serves 6 to 8.

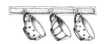

Fantastic Fruit Salad

2 (11 ounce) cans mandarin oranges, drained
2 (15 ounce) cans pineapple chunks, drained
1 (16 ounce) carton frozen strawberries, thawed
1 (20 ounce) can peach pie filling
1 (20 ounce) can apricot pie filling

• In bowl, combine all ingredients.

• Fold mixture gently until they mix well. Serves 12 to 16.

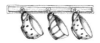

Don't take yourself so seriously. No one else does.

Garden Upside-Down Salad

1 (10 ounce) package mixed spring salad greens
1 cup broccoli florets
1 cup sliced celery
1 red bell pepper, julienned
1 cup sliced zucchini
1 cup sliced baby carrots
Creamy ranch dressing

- In salad bowl, combine all ingredients. Toss with dressing.
  Serves 4 to 6.

Divinity Salad

1 (6 ounce) package lemon gelatin
1 (8 ounce) package cream cheese, softened
¾ cup chopped pecans
1 (15 ounce) can crushed pineapple with juice
1 (8 ounce) carton frozen whipped topping, thawed

- Use mixer to combine gelatin with 1 cup boiling water and mix
  until it dissolves.

- Add cream cheese, beat slowly at first and beat until smooth.
  Add pecans and pineapple.

- Refrigerate until nearly set. Fold in whipped topping and
  pour into 9 x 13-inch dish and refrigerate. Serves 10 to 12.

The sweet potato is one of the most nutritious vegetables we have. It is fat free and cholesterol free, is full of fiber and has significant amounts of vitamins C and E.

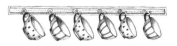

Yummy Butter-Mint Salad

1 (6 ounce) box lime gelatin mix
1 (20 ounce) can crushed pineapple with juice
½ (10 ounce) bag miniature marshmallows
1 (8 ounce) carton frozen whipped topping, thawed
1 (8 ounce) bag butter mints, crushed

* In bowl, pour dry gelatin mix over pineapple. Add marshmallows and set aside overnight.

* Fold in whipped topping and butter mints. Pour into 9 x 13-inch dish and freeze. Serves 8 to 10.

Apple Orchard Salad

1 (10 ounce) package fresh spinach
⅓ cup frozen orange juice concentrate, thawed
¾ cup mayonnaise
1 red apple with peel, diced
5 slices bacon, fried, crumbled

* Tear spinach into small pieces and set aside.

* In bowl, mix orange juice concentrate and mayonnaise and set aside to use as dressing for salad.

* When ready to serve, combine spinach and diced apples in salad bowl.

* Top salad mixture with dressing and crumbled bacon. Serves 6 to 8.

Spinach, Apple and Walnut Salad

6 cups fresh spinach leaves, torn into pieces
2 red delicious apples, cored, chopped
½ cup coarsely chopped walnuts
½ cup wild berry vinaigrette salad dressing

• Combine all ingredients in salad bowl.

• Toss until they mix well. Serves 6 to 8.

Summer Spinach-Fruit Salad

1 (10 ounce) package fresh baby spinach
½ cantaloupe, peeled, cut into bite-size pieces
¾ cup red grapes, halved
½ cup coarsely chopped pecans, toasted
½ cup poppy seed salad dressing

• Combine spinach, cantaloupe, grapes and pecans.

• Toss with dressing. Serves 6 to 8.

TIP: Toast pecans at 275° for 10 minutes.

*The most interesting information comes from
children, for they tell all they know and then stop.*
-Mark Twain

Cheesy Spinach Salad

1 (10 ounce) package baby spinach
1 (9 ounce) package refrigerated cheese tortellini, cooked
¾ cup fresh grated parmesan cheese
1 (8 ounce) bottle poppy seed salad dressing

• In salad bowl, combine spinach, tortellini and cheese and mix well.

• Toss with ¾ cup salad dressing (or more if desired). Serves 8.

Terrific Tortellini Salad

2 (14 ounce) packages frozen cheese tortellini
1 green bell pepper, seeded, diced
1 red bell pepper, seeded, diced
1 cucumber, chopped
1 (14 ounce) can artichoke hearts, rinsed, drained
1 (8 ounce) bottle creamy Caesar salad dressing

• Prepare tortellini according to package directions and drain. Rinse with cold water, drain and refrigerate.

• Combine tortellini and remaining ingredients in large bowl.

• Cover and refrigerate at least 2 hours. Serves 10 to 12.

10 Good Reasons to Have Meals at Home are included in this cookbook. Here's one of them.

5. Family meals teach basic manners and social skills that children must learn to be successful in life. What they learn will help them in new situations and give them more confidence because they will know how to act and what to say and do.

Dressed Black Bean Salad

2 (15 ounce) cans black beans, rinsed, drained
2 ribs celery, chopped
½ bell pepper, julienned
1 small red onion, sliced

• In bowl, combine black beans, celery and bell pepper.
  Separate onion slices into rings and add to bean mixture.

• Toss with salad dressing, cover and refrigerate.

Dressing:

⅓ cup lime juice
2 tablespoons sugar
¼ cup olive oil
¼ teaspoon ground cumin

• Combine dressing ingredients and mix well. Serves 8 to 10.

Zesty Black Bean Salad

1 bunch broccoli, cut into florets
1 cup pitted ripe olives, drained
1 red bell pepper, seeded, julienned
1 (15 ounce) can black beans, rinsed, drained
½ cup zesty Italian salad dressing

• Combine broccoli, olives, bell pepper and beans.

• Toss with dressing. Serves 8 to 10.

Pistachio Salad or Dessert

1 (20 ounce) can crushed pineapple with juice
1 (3 ounce) package instant pistachio pudding mix
2 cups miniature marshmallows
1 cup chopped pecans
1 (8 ounce) carton frozen whipped topping, thawed

• In large bowl, place pineapple and sprinkle with pudding mix. Add marshmallows and pecans. Fold in whipped topping.

• Pour into crystal serving dish. Refrigerate before serving. Serves 10.

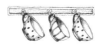

Watergate Salad

1 (20 ounce) can crushed pineapple with juice
2 (3 ounce) packages instant pistachio pudding mix
¾ cup chopped pecans
1 (12 ounce) carton frozen whipped topping, thawed

• In bowl, combine pineapple with pudding mix until it thickens slightly, Add pecans. When mixed well, fold in whipped topping.

• Spoon into glass serving dish and refrigerate 2 to 3 hours before serving. Serves 10 to 12.

A hard thing about business is minding your own.
                              -Anonymous

Easy Chicken Salad

3 cups finely chopped, cooked chicken breasts
1½ cups chopped celery
½ cup sweet pickle relish
2 hard-boiled eggs, chopped
¾ cup mayonnaise

* In bowl, combine all ingredients with several sprinkles of salt
  and pepper. Serves 4 to 6.

*TIP: Add ½ cup pecans if you have them. They add a special crunchy
texture to salad.*

Fluffy Deviled Eggs

8 eggs, hard-boiled
¼ teaspoon dried parsley
¼ teaspoon tarragon
¼ teaspoon dill weed
½ cup finely shredded mozzarella cheese
¼ cup finely chopped pecans
¼ - ⅓ cup creamy dijon-style mayonnaise

* Cut eggs in half lengthwise, remove yolks and set aside
  14 whites. Add 2 remaining whites to egg yolks (for more
  filling) and mash.

* Add parsley, tarragon, dill, cheese, pecans and enough
  mayonnaise to make mixture creamy. Mix with fork for
  fluffy texture.

* Fill each egg white with fluffy yolk mixture. Refrigerate.
  Serves 8 to 12.

*Why do you put bells on cows? Because the
horns don't work.*

Nifty Beef Spread for Sandwiches

1 (5 ounce) jar dried beef, chopped
1 (8 ounce) carton sour cream
¾ cup shredded Swiss or cheddar cheese

• In bowl, combine all ingredients and mix well.

• Cover and refrigerate.

• Spread on white bread with crusts removed and cut into finger sandwiches. Serves 3 to 4.

Spinach Sandwich Spread

1 (10 ounce) package frozen chopped spinach, thawed, well drained
1 cup mayonnaise
1 (8 ounce) carton sour cream
½ cup finely minced onion
1 (1 ounce) package vegetable soup mix

• Drain spinach on several paper towels. In bowl, combine all ingredients and mix well.

• Refrigerate for 3 to 4 hours before making sandwiches.

• Use thin white bread for sandwiches. Yields 2 cups.

I think age is a very high price to pay for maturity.
                              -Tom Stoppard

Cherry-Cheese Sandwich Spread

1 (8 ounce) jar maraschino cherries
1 (8 ounce) package cream cheese, softened
½ cup finely chopped pecans

- Drain cherries and dice very fine.

- In mixing bowl, beat cream cheese until creamy and combine with chopped cherries and pecans. Mix well.

- Trim crusts from several slices white bread, banana-nut bread, etc.

- Use filling for open-face sandwiches or make into 3-layered ribbon sandwiches. Serves 2 to 4.

Olive-Egg Salad Sandwich Spread

6 hard-boiled eggs
12 stuffed green olives, finely chopped
Mayonnaise

- Rinse hard-boiled eggs in cool water, peel shells and chop.

- In bowl, combine eggs, olives and enough mayonnaise to moisten.

- Refrigerate until ready to use.

- Spread on wheat bread and cut in half for sandwiches. Serves 4.

TIP: This spread is also good with ½ cup chopped pecans added.

Easy Chicken-Almond Sandwich

2 cups finely shredded, cooked chicken
½ cup finely chopped almonds, toasted
Mayonnaise

- In bowl, combine chicken and almonds with enough mayonnaise to moisten and form spread.

- For sandwiches, spread chicken filling on thinly sliced, white bread. Remove crusts.

- Cut into squares, triangles or bars. Serves 3 to 4.

TIP: You may also stir ½ cup finely diced celery.

Simple Hot Bunwiches

8 hamburger buns
8 slices Swiss cheese
8 slices ham
8 slices turkey
8 slices American cheese

- Lay out all 8 buns. On bottom bun slice, place Swiss cheese, ham, turkey and American cheese. Place top bun slice over American cheese.

- Wrap each bunwich individually in foil and place in freezer.

- When ready to serve, remove from freezer 2 to 3 hours before serving.

- Heat bunwich at 325° for about 30 minutes and serve hot. Serves 8.

Open-Face Roast Beef Sandwich

This is great for leftover roast.

Thick slices Texas toast bread, toasted
Roast beef spread
Shredded lettuce
Tomatoes, chopped, drained
Sliced ripe olives

Roast Beef Spread:

1½ cups slivered roast beef
⅓ cup drained sweet relish
2 hard-boiled eggs, chopped
⅓ cup chopped pecans
⅓ - ½ cup mayonnaise

- Combine roast beef spread ingredients except mayonnaise and mix well. Fold in just enough mayonnaise to hold mixture without being too creamy.

- Place 1 slice toast on serving plate and pile about 3 tablespoons roast beef spread. Top with shredded lettuce, tomatoes and ripe olives. Serves 2 to 4.

Deviled Ham Spread

1 (4½) ounce) can deviled ham
⅓ cup sour cream
⅓ cup shredded cheddar cheese

- Combine all ingredients and mix well. Serve with crackers or use as sandwich spread. Serves 2.

Thyme Roasted Asparagus

2 bunches fresh asparagus, trimmed
3 tablespoons olive oil
¾ teaspoon dried thyme

- Preheat oven to 400°. Place asparagus in baking dish lined with foil. Drizzle with oil and thyme and toss to coat. Sprinkle with a little salt and pepper.

- Bake uncovered for 15 minutes. Serves 8 to 10.

Parmesan Baked Onions

4 yellow onions
¼ cup (½ stick) butter, cut into small pieces
½ - 1 teaspoon seasoned black pepper
1 cup finely shredded parmesan cheese

- Preheat oven to 400°. Peel onions, leave ends intact and place onion on 12-inch piece of foil (cut slice off bottom of onion so it will sit evenly). Cut onion into eighths but not through to root end. Pull up foil slightly around onion.

- Press butter and cheese evenly into onion separations and sprinkle with salt and seasoned pepper. Pull foil completely around onion and arrange in 7 x 11-inch baking pan. Bake for 1 hour. Serves 4.

The noblest of all dogs is the hot dog. It feeds the hand that bites it.
                                    -Lawrence J. Peter

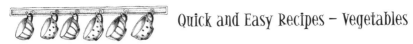

Cheesy Baked Cabbage

1 head cabbage
½ red bell pepper, chopped
1 (10 ounce) can cream of celery soup
1 (8 ounce) package shredded 4-cheese blend

- Preheat oven to 325°. Cut cabbage in chunks and layer in sprayed 7 x 11-inch baking dish with bell pepper, soup and cheese.

- Cover and bake for 45 minutes. Serves 6 to 8.

Creamy Baked Cauliflower

1 medium cauliflower, broken into florets
1 cup dry, seasoned breadcrumbs, divided
1 cup half and half cream
2 tablespoons (¼ stick) butter, cut into slices
Fresh parsley

- Preheat oven to 350°. In saucepan, combine cauliflower, ½ cup water and 1 teaspoon salt and bring to boil. Reduce heat, cover and cook for 6 minutes or until cauliflower is barely tender-crisp. Drain.

- Sprinkle ¼ cup breadcrumbs in sprayed 2-quart baking dish. Add drained cauliflower, cream and dot with butter slices.

- Sprinkle remaining breadcrumbs over top and bake uncovered for 25 to 20 minutes.

- Garnish with fresh parsley. Serves 6.

Oven-Fried Cauliflower

1 medium cauliflower, broken into florets
1 cup mayonnaise
1½ cups dry, Italian-seasoned breadcrumbs

- Preheat oven to 350°. Spoon mayonnaise into large, resealable plastic bag and add cauliflower. Seal and shake to coat.

- Place breadcrumbs in separate plastic bag and add half florets. Shake to coat and spread in sprayed baking pan. Repeat with remaining florets.

- Bake for 1 hour. Serves 6.

Cauliflower Medley

1 head cauliflower, cut into florets
1 (15 ounce) can Italian stewed tomatoes
1 bell pepper, chopped
1 onion, chopped
¼ cup (½ stick) butter
1 cup shredded cheddar cheese

- In large saucepan, place cauliflower, stewed tomatoes, bell pepper, onion and butter.

- Add about 2 tablespoons water and a little salt and pepper.

- Cook in covered saucepan for 10 to 15 minutes or until cauliflower is done. Do not let cauliflower get mushy.

- Place in 2-quart casserole, sprinkle cheese on top and bake at 350° just until cheese melts. Serves 6.

Cream-Style Carrots

¼ cup (½ stick) butter
3 tablespoons flour
1½ cups milk
2 (15 ounce) cans sliced carrots

- Melt butter in saucepan and add flour plus ½ teaspoon salt and mix well. Over medium heat, cook milk and stir constantly. Heat until mixture is thick.

- In smaller saucepan, heat carrots and drain. Add carrots to cream mixture and serve hot. Serves 8.

Honey-Glazed Carrots

1 (16 ounce) package fresh, baby carrots
¼ cup (½ stick) butter
⅓ cup honey
2 teaspoons lemon juice
¼ teaspoon ground ginger

- In saucepan cook carrots with ⅓ cup water for 8 minutes. Drain well.

- In skillet, combine butter and honey and cook until ingredients blend thoroughly. Add lemon juice and ginger and stir.

- Combine heated mixture with carrots and heat thoroughly. Stir well to glaze carrots. Serves 6.

Farmer John's Creamy Sweet Corn

1 (16 ounce) package frozen whole kernel corn
¼ cup (½ stick) butter
¼ cup half-and-half cream
1 tablespoon sugar

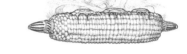

- In saucepan, combine all ingredients plus ½ teaspoon salt and bring to boil.

- Reduce heat and simmer uncovered for 8 to 10 minutes or until liquid evaporates. Serves 4.

South-of-the-Border Corn Bake

3 (15 ounce) cans whole kernel corn, drained
1 (10 ounce) can cream of corn soup
1 (16 ounce) jar salsa, divided
1 (8 ounce) package shredded Mexican 4-cheese blend, divided

- Preheat oven to 350°. In large bowl, combine corn, soup, 1 cup salsa and half cheese. Mix well and pour into sprayed 2-quart baking dish. Bake for 25 to 20 minutes or until bubbly on sides.

- Remove from oven, sprinkle remaining cheese and heat an additional 3 or 4 minutes.

- Serve with remaining salsa. Serves 10 to 12.

I sought my soul, but my soul I could not see;
I sought my God, but my God eluded me;
I sought my brother – and found all three.
–Anonymous

Green Bean Bake

1 (10 ounce) can cream of mushroom soup
½ cup milk
1 teaspoon soy sauce
2 (15 ounce) cans cut green beans, drained
1½ cups French-fried onions

- Preheat oven to 350°. In saucepan, combine soup, milk and soy sauce and heat until ingredients mix well. Add green beans and ⅔ cup fried onions.

- Spoon mixture into sprayed 2-quart baking dish and bake for 25 minutes.

- Remove from oven, sprinkle remaining fried onions and bake for another 10 minutes. Serves 8 to 10.

Green Bean Casserole Twist

2 (15 ounce) cans green beans, drained
1 (10 ounce) can cream of celery soup
1 cup crushed potato chips

- Combine green beans and soup and pour into sprayed 2-quart casserole dish.

- Top with crushed potato chips and bake at 350° for 25 to 30 minutes. Serves 8 to 10.

Help thy brother's boat across and lo! thine has reached the shore.

–Old Hindu Proverb

Green Peas Casserole

2 (10 ounce) packages frozen green peas
1 cup shredded cheddar cheese
1 (10 ounce) can golden mushroom soup

• Cook peas according to package directions and drain.

• Combine peas, cheese and soup and bake in sprayed casserole dish at 350° for 30 to 35 minutes. Serves 8.

Mama's Lemon Snap Peas

3 tablespoons butter
1 (16 ounce) package frozen snap peas, trimmed
1 teaspoon grated lemon zest
1 teaspoon fresh thyme

• In skillet over medium heat, melt butter and add peas. Saute 3 minutes and stir constantly.

• Add lemon zest and thyme. Cook an additional minute or until peas are tender-crisp. Serves 6.

I would rather try to carry 10 plastic grocery bags in each hand than take two trips to bring in my groceries.

Fast Snow Peas

1½ pounds fresh snow peas
1 tablespoon lemon juice
3 tablespoons butter

- Cook peas in steamer for 3 to 4 minutes.

- Season with lemon juice, butter and salt to taste.
  Serves 6 to 8.

French Onion-Rice Casserole

1 (10 ounce) can French onion soup
1 cup regular rice (not instant)
½ cup chopped celery

- In bowl, combine all ingredients with 1 cup water. Mix well.

- Cook in covered saucepan over medium heat for 25 to
  30 minutes or until rice is tender. Fluff with fork. Serves 6.

*Nothing feels exactly like the moment during an
argument when you realize you are wrong.*

Fancy Caramelized Onions

These onions add an elegant touch when served with beef roast, baked potatoes, burgers, grilled chicken or steak.

2 large onions, cut in ¼-inch slices
1 tablespoon oil
1½ teaspoons sugar
2 tablespoons balsamic vinaigrette salad dressing

- In large skillet over low to medium heat, cook onions in oil for 25 minutes. Stir occasionally. Add sugar and cook for another 4 minutes or until golden brown.

- Drizzle with dressing just before serving. Serves 4 to 6.

Broccoli-Cheese Potato Topper

1 (10 ounce) can nacho cheese soup
2 tablespoons sour cream
½ teaspoon dijon-style mustard
1 (10 ounce) box frozen broccoli
  florets, cooked
4 medium potatoes, baked, fluffed

- In 1-quart microwave-safe baking dish, stir soup, sour cream, mustard and broccoli.

- Heat mixture in microwave for 2 to 2½ minutes.

- Remove from heat and spoon over potato halves. Serves 6 to 8.

Roasted Cheddar-Potato Bake

1 (7 ounce) box roasted garlic mashed potato mix
1 (8 ounce) carton sour cream
1½ cups shredded cheddar cheese, divided
1 (3 ounce) can cheddar French-fried onions

- Preheat oven to 375°. Prepare 2 potato pouches according to package directions. While hot, stir in sour cream and 1 cup cheese and mix well.

- Spoon into sprayed 2-quart baking dish and sprinkle with remaining cheese and fried onions.

- Bake 10 minutes or until casserole is hot and fried onions are golden. Serves 8.

Parsley New Potatoes

3 pounds small, new potatoes
¾ cup (1½ sticks) butter, melted
6 tablespoons minced parsley

- In pan, cook small, new potatoes in 5 cups boiling water until tender and drain.

- Sprinkle with melted butter and minced parsley

- Serve hot. Serves 8 to 10.

The secret of staying young is to live honestly, eat slowly and lie about your age.
-Lucille Ball

Crumbly Hash Browns

1 (10 ounce) can cream of onion soup
1 (10 ounce) can cream of celery soup
1 (30 ounce) package frozen shredded hash browns, thawed
1 (8 ounce) package shredded Mexican 4-cheese blend, divided
2 cups crushed corn flakes

- Preheat oven to 350°. In large bowl, combine soups, hash browns and half cheese and mix well. Spoon into sprayed 9 x 13-inch casserole dish.

- Sprinkle mixture with remaining cheese and corn flakes. Bake uncovered for 45 minutes. Serves 10 to 12.

Creamy Potatoes au Gratin

1 (16 ounce) package frozen, shredded hash browns, thawed
1 (8 ounce) carton whipping cream
1 (8 ounce) package shredded cheddar-colby cheese, divided
4 fresh green onions, chopped

- Preheat oven to 350°. In large bowl, combine hash browns, whipping cream, half cheese, green onions plus generous amount of salt and pepper. Mix well.

- Transfer mixture to sprayed 7 x 11-inch baking dish. Bake 25 minutes or until hot and bubbly.

- Sprinkle remaining cheese on top and return to oven for additional 5 minutes. Serves 10 to 12.

New Potatoes and Lemon-Butter

3 pounds small new (red) potatoes

- Peel only a few strips of skin from around each potato. Place potatoes in pot of boiling water and cook 20 minutes or until tender.

- Remove when done and place in bowl.

Lemon-Butter Sauce:

½ cup (1 stick) butter
¼ cup olive oil
3 tablespoons minced fresh parsley
⅓ cup lemon juice
¼ teaspoon nutmeg

- In saucepan, combine all sauce ingredients and bring to boil.

- Remove from heat and drizzle mixture over new potatoes in bowl.

- Toss to coat well. Serves 8 to 10.

Rice Bake Inspiration

1 (10 ounce) can cream of onion soup
1 (10 ounce) can beef broth
¼ cup (½ stick) butter, melted
1 cup rice

- Preheat oven to 350°. In bowl, combine soup, broth, and butter plus a little salt and pepper. Pour into sprayed 7 x 11-inch baking dish and cover with foil.

- Bake 30 minutes, remove from oven and stir in rice. Cook for additional 30 minutes. Serves 6 to 8.

Carnival Couscous

*This is a delicious, colorful dish that
easily replaces rice or vegetable.*

1 (6 ounce) box herbed chicken couscous
¼ cup (½ stick) butter
1 red bell pepper, seeded, minced
1 yellow squash, seeded, minced
¾ cup finely chopped, fresh broccoli florets

- Cook couscous according to package directions but leave out butter.

- Add butter to saucepan and saute bell pepper, squash and broccoli. Cook about 10 minutes or until vegetables are almost tender.

- Combine heated vegetable mixture with couscous. Serves 8.

*TIP: If you want to do this a little ahead of time, place couscous and
vegetable in sprayed non-stick baking dish and heat at 325° for
about 20 minutes.*

No-Fuss Pesto for Pasta

3 cups fresh basil leaves, washed, dried
½ cup zesty Italian salad dressing
⅓ cup grated parmesan cheese

- Combine all ingredients in mixing bowl and process until smooth with blender. Cover and refrigerate. Yields 1 to 1½ cups.

TIP: Combine pesto with your favorite pasta.

E-Z Ricotta Pasta

1 (16 ounce) package penne pasta
¼ cup (½ stick) butter
1½ cups ricotta cheese
1 cup grated parmesan cheese
1 tablespoon dried parsley

- Preheat oven to 350°. Cook pasta according to package directions and drain. While hot, stir in remaining ingredients plus a little salt and pepper.

- Pour into sprayed 2½-quart baking dish and cover. Bake for 10 minutes or until bubbly hot. Serves 8.

Tomato-Basil Penne Pasta

1 (8 ounce) package penne pasta
1 (8 ounce) carton fresh mushrooms, sliced
3 tablespoons extra virgin olive oil, divided
1 (15 ounce) can Italian stewed tomatoes
1 teaspoon dried basil
½ cup crumbled feta cheese

- Cook pasta according to package directions and drain well. Add 1 tablespoon olive oil to large skillet and saute mushrooms. Add tomatoes, basil and a little salt. Cook and stir for 10 minutes.

- Stir remaining oil into pasta and fold in skillet with tomatoes. Cook for 5 minutes or until it heats thoroughly. Stir in feta cheese. Serve hot. Serves 8.

Cheese Ravioli and Zucchini

1 (25 ounce) package fresh cheese-filled ravioli
4 small zucchini, sliced
2 ribs celery, sliced diagonally
1 (16 ounce) jar marinara sauce
¼ cup grated parmesan cheese

- Cook ravioli according to package directions and drain.
  Return to saucepan and keep warm. (You can also use frozen
  chicken ravioli.)

- Place zucchini and celery in another saucepan and pour
  marinara sauce over vegetables. Cook and stir over medium-
  high heat for about 8 minutes or until vegetables are
  tender-crisp. Spoon marinara-vegetable mixture over ravioli
  and toss gently. Pour into serving bowl and garnish with
  parmesan. Serves 6.

Sauteed-Pepper Linguine

1 (10 ounce) package linguine
3 tablespoons extra virgin olive oil
2 red bell peppers, seeded, julienned
1 cup chopped onion
1 cup sliced mushrooms
2 teaspoons minced garlic

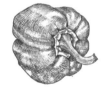

- Cook linguine according to package directions and drain. Add
  olive oil to skillet and saute bell peppers, onion and mushrooms.

- Stir pepper-mushroom mixture into linguine and heat. Stir
  gently until mixture is hot. Serves 6.

Sometimes bad decisions make good stories.

3-Cheese Macaroni

1 cup macaroni
1½ cups small curd cottage cheese, drained
1¼ cups shredded cheddar or American cheese
¼ cup grated parmesan cheese

- Preheat oven to 350°.

- Cook macaroni according to package directions in saucepan and drain.

- Combine cottage cheese and cheeses in bowl. Add macaroni to cheese mixture.

- Spoon into sprayed 2-quart baking dish. Cover and bake for 35 minutes. Serves 4 to 6.

Seasoned Pasta

2 (14 ounce) cans seasoned chicken broth with Italian herbs
3 cups corkscrew pasta
½ - 1 cup grated parmesan cheese

- Heat broth in saucepan until it boils and stir in pasta.

- Reduce heat, simmer until pasta is fork-tender and stir often.

- Pour into serving bowl and sprinkle with cheese. Serves 8 to 10.

Sausage Dressing

1 (6 ounce) box herb stuffing mix
1 pound bulk pork sausage
1 cup chopped onion

- Prepare stuffing according to package directions.

- In skillet, brown sausage and drain well. Saute onion in skillet drippings.

- In bowl, combine stuffing mix, sausage and onions and mix well.

- Pour into sprayed casserole dish and bake at 325° for 30 minutes. Serves 8 to 10.

Sausage-Rice Casserole

1 pound pork sausage
3 cups cooked rice
1 (10 ounce) can golden cream of mushroom soup

- Fry sausage in skillet, crumble and drain.

- In bowl, combine all ingredients and mix well.

- Pour into sprayed casserole dish and bake at 350° for 30 minutes. Serves 8.

What is the best way to communicate with a fish?
Drop it a line.

Yankee Doodle Macaroni

1 (16 ounce) package spiral macaroni
¼ cup (½ stick) butter
1 (16 ounce) package shredded cheddar cheese
2 cups carton milk

- Preheat oven to 375°. In saucepan, cook macaroni for about 4 minutes less than package directions indicate. Drain well.

- Spoon one-third macaroni into sprayed 9 x 13-inch baking dish. Sprinkle a little salt and black pepper, dot with one-third butter cut into small chunks and top with one-third cheese. Repeat this process twice. (Do not press down on layers.)

- Pour milk slowly over macaroni-cheese mixture, cover and bake for 1 hour. Serves 8 to 10.

The War of Independence inspired quilters to create patriotic-themed quilts. If a loved one was killed, a "Memorial Quilt" constructed from the deceased's clothing helped ease the pain.

Catalina Chicken

1 cup apricot preserves
1 (8 ounce) bottle catalina salad dressing
1 (1 ounce) package onion soup mix
6 - 8 boneless, skinless chicken breast halves

- In bowl, combine apricot preserves, dressing and soup mix.

- Place chicken breasts in large, sprayed baking dish and pour apricot mixture over chicken. (For change of pace, use Russian dressing instead of Catalina).

- Bake uncovered at 325° for 1 hour 20 minutes.

- Serve over hot rice. Serves 6 to 8.

Dressed Artichoke-Chicken Bake

1 (14 ounce) jar artichoke hearts, drained, chopped
¾ cup mayonnaise
1 (8 ounce) package cubed Velveeta® cheese, divided
6 boneless, skinless chicken breast halves

- Preheat oven to 350°. In bowl, combine artichokes, mayonnaise and half cheese and mix well.

- Place chicken in sprayed 9 x 13-inch baking dish and spread artichoke mixture over each chicken breast.

- Bake uncovered for 40 minutes. Remove from oven, place remaining cheese cubes over chicken and cook for another 10 minutes. Serve over hot cooked rice. Serves 6.

Baked Buttermilk Chicken

1 whole chicken
½ cup buttermilk
1 cup dry, Italian-seasoned breadcrumbs

- Cut chicken into serving-size pieces.

- Dip chicken in buttermilk and roll in breadcrumbs.

- Place on sprayed 9 x 13-inch baking dish and bake at 350° for 1 hour or until tender. Serves 6.

TIP: If you don't want to cut up a chicken, buy the pieces you want. It's much easier.

Baked Mexican Chicken

4 - 6 boneless, skinless chicken breast halves
1 (1 ounce) package taco seasoning mix
1 (10 ounce) can enchilada sauce
Corn tortillas

- Place chicken in sprayed 9 x 13-inch baking dish. Sprinkle desired amount of taco seasoning mix over chicken.

- Pour enchilada sauce over chicken and bake at 350° for 1 hour or until tender.

- Serve with warmed corn tortillas. Serves 4 to 6.

It is only great souls that know how much glory there is in being good.
-Sophocles

Broccoli-Cheese Chicken

Vegetable oil
4 boneless, skinless chicken breast halves
1 (10 ounce) can broccoli-cheese soup
1 (16 ounce) package frozen broccoli florets
½ cup milk
Cooked rice

- In skillet with a little oil, cook chicken 15 minutes or until brown on both sides, remove and set aside. In same skillet, combine soup, broccoli, milk and a little pepper and heat to boiling. Return chicken to skillet and reduce heat to low.

- Cover and cook for 25 minutes or until chicken is no longer pink and broccoli is tender. Serve over rice. Serves 4.

Ritzy Baked Chicken

4 boneless, skinless chicken breast halves
1 cup sour cream
1 cup Cheez-It® crackers, crushed

- Roll chicken breasts in sour cream and crushed crackers.

- Bake at 325° for 1 hour or until tender. Serves 4.

During the first 150 years of quilting in the colonies, swapping pieces of fabric was as popular as swapping recipes. Variety in fabrics and colors were not universally available and travelers always carried treasures of fabrics to trade.

Ranch-Style Chicken

2 eggs, well-beaten
1 (8 ounce) package cornbread muffin mix
1 (1 ounce) package ranch-style salad dressing mix
6 boneless, skinless chicken breast halves

- In shallow bowl, combine eggs and $\frac{1}{4}$ cup water. In separate bowl, combine cornbread and dressing mixes.

- Dip chicken breasts in egg mixture and then muffin-dressing mixture.

- In large skillet with a little oil, fry chicken breasts over medium to high heat. Cook on each side about 8 minutes or until juices run clear. Serves 6.

Crusty Baked Chicken

8 skinless chicken thighs
1 large egg
2$\frac{1}{2}$ cups corn flakes, crushed
$\frac{1}{2}$ teaspoon cayenne pepper

- Preheat oven to 400°. Rinse chicken, pat dry with paper towels and sprinkle generously with salt.

- In bowl, whisk egg with 1 tablespoon water. In separate bowl, combine crushed corn flakes and cayenne pepper.

- Coat chicken pieces in egg mixture and then seasoned corn flakes. Press chicken firmly in flakes so they adhere well. Place pieces in sprayed 9 x 13-inch baking dish and arrange so they do not touch. Bake uncovered 30 minutes or until golden brown and crisp. Serves 6.

Crispy Rosemary Chicken

1 cup grape nut cereal
1 teaspoon garlic salt
¾ teaspoon dried rosemary leaves, crushed
4 - 5 boneless, skinless chicken breast halves

- Preheat oven to 400°. Place cereal in blender, cover and crush finely. In shallow bowl, mix with garlic salt, rosemary and a little black pepper.

- Dry chicken with paper towels and brush a little oil on each piece. Dip each piece in cereal-seasoning mix and place on sprayed 10 x 15-inch baking pan. Arrange pieces so they do not touch.

- Bake for 25 minutes or until chicken cooks well and is light brown. Serves 4 to 5.

Easy Orange-Onion Chicken

4 boneless, skinless chicken breasts
1 cup orange juice
1 (1 ounce) package dry onion soup mix

- Trim any visible fat on chicken. Arrange chicken pieces in sprayed 9 x 13-inch baking dish. Pour orange juice over chicken and sprinkle with soup mix.

- Bake at 350° for 30 minutes. Turn chicken and bake for 30 minutes longer or until tender. Serves 4.

Cornish Hen a la Orange

4 (18 ounce) cornish hens, rinsed, dried
3 tablespoons butter, melted
1 (10 ounce) jar orange marmalade

- Place hens in sprayed, large baking pan.

- In bowl, combine melted butter and orange marmalade and set aside.

- Bake hens at 350° for 30 minutes.

- Pour orange mixture over them and bake for 1 hour longer. Baste several times. Serves 4 to 8.

Orange-Glazed Chicken

½ cup orange marmalade, divided
4 - 5 boneless, skinless chicken breast halves
1 (1 ounce) package chicken-seasoned coating mix
¼ cup Italian salad dressing

- Preheat oven to 400°. Spread 3 tablespoons marmalade over chicken breasts. Pour coating mix in shallow dish and dip chicken to coat both sides.

- Place chicken in sprayed 9 x 13-inch baking dish and bake for 25 minutes.

- In bowl, combine dressing and remaining marmalade. Heat and spoon mixtures over chicken before serving. Serve chicken over fresh baby spinach or hot cooked rice. Serves 4 to 5.

Lemon Chicken over Rice

Marinade:

$\frac{1}{3}$ cup lemon juice
$\frac{1}{4}$ cup soy sauce
3 tablespoons extra virgin olive oil
2 teaspoons prepared minced garlic

- In large, resealable plastic bag, combine all marinade ingredients and add chicken breasts. Seal bag and turn to coat. Refrigerate 8 hours or overnight.

Chicken:

6 boneless, skinless chicken breast halves
$\frac{1}{2}$ cup chicken broth
2 tablespoons cornstarch
$\frac{1}{4}$ cup sesame seeds, toasted

- Remove chicken from marinade and place on sprayed broiler pan. Set marinade aside and broil chicken 12 to 15 minutes. Turn once.

- While chicken broils, strain marinade and place in saucepan with cornstarch, broth and $\frac{1}{2}$ cup water. Bring to boil and stir constantly until mixture is thick. Pour marinade over chicken breasts.

- Sprinkle with sesame seeds and serve over hot, cooked rice. Serves 6.

An excellent health tip: Smile and Laugh More.

Lemon-Roasted Chicken

Marinade:

$\frac{1}{3}$ cup extra virgin olive oil
$\frac{1}{3}$ cup lemon juice
$\frac{1}{3}$ cup white wine or chicken broth
2 teaspoons fresh chopped rosemary
2 teaspoons fresh thyme
1 teaspoon prepared minced garlic

Chicken:

1 (3 - 3$\frac{1}{2}$ pounds) whole chicken

- Preheat oven to 375°. Combine all marinade ingredients in large, resealable plastic bag. (If using dried herbs rather than fresh, use $\frac{1}{2}$ teaspoon each of rosemary and thyme.) Reserve $\frac{1}{3}$ cup marinade and refrigerate.

- Add chicken to marinade in plastic bag and refrigerate for 2 hours. Turn several times.

- Place chicken in roasting pan with breast side up and tuck wing tips under. Brush chicken with reserved marinade and bake for 1 hour. Baste several times.

- Set aside chicken for 15 minutes for easier carving. Serves 6 to 8.

Happy is he with such a mother!
–Alfred Lord Tennyson

Chicken Mozzarella

6 boneless, skinless chicken breast halves
½ (28 ounce) jar spaghetti sauce
6 slices mozzarella cheese

- Place chicken breasts in sprayed 9 x 13-inch baking dish and cover with spaghetti sauce. Bake covered at 325° for 1 hour.

- Remove from oven and top each breast with 1 slice cheese. Return to oven and bake uncovered for 10 minutes longer.

- Serve with spaghetti or noodles, if desired. Serves 6.

Chipper Chicken

1 (3 pound) chicken
½ cup (1 stick) butter, melted
3 cup potato chips, crushed

- Cut chicken into serving-size pieces.

- Dip chicken in melted butter and roll in crushed potato chips.

- Pour into sprayed 9 x 13-inch pan and bake at 350° for 1 hour or until tender. Serves 8.

TIP: If you don't want to cut up chicken, buy the pieces you want. It's much easier.

Keep the dream alive – hit the snooze button.

Favorite Chicken Breasts

6 - 8 boneless, skinless chicken breast halves
1 (10 ounce) can cream of mushroom soup
¾ cup white wine or white cooking wine
1 (8 ounce) carton sour cream

• Place chicken breasts in large, shallow baking pan and sprinkle a little salt and pepper. Bake uncovered at 350° for 30 minutes.

• In saucepan, combine soup, wine and sour cream and heat just enough to mix.

• Remove chicken from oven and pour sour cream mixture over chicken.

• Return to oven to cook another 30 minutes. Baste twice and serve over rice. Serves 6 to 8.

Pepper-Jack Chicken

1 (4 ounce) piece pepper jack cheese
4 boneless, skinless chicken breast halves
1 tablespoon taco seasoning
Oil

• Preheat oven to 350°. Cut cheese into 4 strips. Flatten chicken to ¼-inch thickness. Place strip of cheese down center of each chicken breast, fold chicken over cheese and secure with toothpicks. Rub each chicken roll with taco seasoning.

• In skillet with a little oil, brown chicken on all sides and place in sprayed 7 x 11-inch baking dish. Bake uncovered for 25 minutes or until juices run clear. Serves 4.

Party Chicken Breasts

6 - 8 boneless, skinless chicken breast halves
8 strips bacon
1 (2 ounce) jar chipped beef
1 (10 ounce) can cream of chicken soup
1 (8 ounce) carton sour cream

- Wrap each chicken breast with 1 strip bacon and secure with toothpick.

- Place chipped beef in bottom of large, shallow baking pan. Top with chicken.

- In saucepan, combine soup and sour cream and heat.

- Pour mixture over chicken and bake uncovered at 325° for 1 hour. Serves 6 to 8.

Southwest-Ranchero Chicken

2 (10 ounce) cans creamy tomato soup
3 cups cubed, deli chicken or turkey
8 (8-inch) corn tortillas, cut into strips
1 (8 ounce) package Mexican 4-cheese blend, divided

- Preheat oven to 350°. In large bowl, combine soup, chicken, tortilla strips, half cheese plus $\frac{2}{3}$ cup water. Spoon into sprayed 9 x 13-inch baking dish.

- Cover and bake for 25 minutes. Uncover, sprinkle remaining cheese and return to oven for 5 minutes. Serves 8.

Irish Chicken

1 (2½ pound) chicken
1 egg, beaten
1½ cups dry potato flakes

- Cut chicken into serving-size pieces.

- Dip each chicken piece in egg and roll in potato flakes. Repeat with all chicken pieces.

- Melt butter in shallow baking pan, place chicken in pan and bake at 375° for 30 minutes.

- Turn chicken over and bake for 20 minutes more. Serves 6.

TIP: If you don't want to cut up chicken, buy the pieces you want. It's much easier.

Easy Barbecued Chicken

4 - 6 boneless, skinless chicken breast halves
½ cup ketchup
1 (12 ounce) can cola soda

- Cook chicken in large sprayed skillet.

- In bowl, combine ketchup and cola and mix well. Pour mixture over chicken and cook at 350° for about 1 hour or until tender. Serves 4 to 6.

Parmesan Chicken

1 (28 ounce) jar spaghetti sauce
6 tablespoons grated parmesan cheese, divided
6 boneless, skinless chicken breast halves
1 (8 ounce) package shredded mozzarella cheese

- Preheat oven to 375°. Pour spaghetti sauce into 9 x 13-inch baking dish and stir in 4 tablespoons parmesan cheese. Place chicken breasts in dish and turn over to coat both sides with sauce. Cover with foil and bake for 35 minutes.

- Uncover and sprinkle mozzarella and remaining parmesan cheese.

- Cook 5 minutes or until cheese melts. Serve over hot cooked rice or pasta. Serves 6.

Special Sunday Chicken

4 boneless, skinless chicken breast halves
1 (10 ounce) can cream of mushroom soup
1½ cups shredded cheddar cheese

- Place chicken in sprayed 9 x 13-inch dish and bake at 350° for 30 minutes.

- Remove from oven and spread soup over chicken. Top with cheese.

- Bake 30 minutes longer. Serves 4.

Cotton Pickin' Pizza Chicken

4 boneless, skinless chicken breast halves
1 (14 ounce) jar pasta sauce
¾ cup pepperoni slices
1 cup shredded mozzarella cheese

- Preheat oven to 350°. In skillet with a little oil, brown chicken until no longer pink and place in sprayed 7 x 11-inch baking dish. Pour pasta sauce over chicken, cover and cook for 20 minutes.

- Uncover and place pepperoni slices over each chicken piece. Sprinkle cheese over top and return to oven for 5 minutes or until cheese melts.

- Serve with hot cooked pasta. Serves 4.

Super Party Chicken

1 (2 ounce) package dried beef, sliced
4 boneless, skinless chicken breast halves
2 (10 ounce) cans cream of mushroom soup

- Spread dried beef slices in sprayed 9 x 13-inch baking dish. Place chicken over beef.

- Pour mushroom soup over chicken and refrigerate for 3 hours.

- Bake at 275° for 2 hours 30 minutes or until chicken is tender. Serves 4.

TIP: Sometimes I chop dried beef, mix with soup and pour over chicken before baking. Sometimes I do not refrigerate before baking. It's great either way. I serve with wild rice, salad and green beans.

Spice Island-Glazed Chicken

½ cup Italian salad dressing
1 teaspoon ground ginger
1 whole fryer chicken, quartered
⅓ cup peach preserves

- In shallow bowl, combine dressing and ginger and mix. Add chicken and turn to coat well. Cover and marinate in refrigerator 3 to 5 hours.

- Remove chicken, reserve ¼ cup marinade and boil 1 minute. Add preserves and stir until they melt. Broil chicken until it is no longer pink.

- Brush chicken with preserve mixture during last 5 minutes of cooking. Serves 4 to 6.

Rosemary's Chicken

5 boneless, skinless chicken breast halves
1 onion, finely chopped
1 tablespoon minced garlic
1 tablespoon fresh rosemary leaves
1 (8 ounce) carton marinara sauce

- Preheat oven to 375°. Arrange chicken breasts in sprayed 9 x 13-inch baking dish.

- In small skillet with a little oil, saute onion 5 minutes over low heat. Add garlic, rosemary, marinara sauce and ½ cup water and mix well. Spoon over chicken pieces and bake uncovered 35 to 40 minutes. Baste twice during cooking time.

- Serve chicken on platter and spoon sauce over top. Serves 5.

Special Chicken-Beef Combo

1 (2 ounce) jar sliced dried beef
6 - 8 boneless, skinless chicken breast halves
1 (10 ounce) can nacho cheese soup
1 (8 ounce) carton sour cream

- Preheat oven to 350°. Arrange beef slices evenly in sprayed 9 x 13-inch baking dish. Place chicken breasts over beef slices.

- In bowl, combine soup, sour cream and ¼ cup water and mix well. Spoon mixture over chicken and bake uncovered for 35 minutes.

- Serve over hot cooked rice or pasta. Serves 6 to 8.

Roasted Teriyaki Chicken

¾ cup roasted garlic-teriyaki marinade
2 tablespoons packed brown sugar
2 tablespoons oil
6 boneless, skinless chicken breast halves

- In bowl, combine marinade, brown sugar and oil. Pour into large, resealable plastic bag and add chicken breasts. Press air out of bag and close securely. Refrigerate for 2 to 4 hours. Turn bag several times to coat chicken well.

- Remove chicken from bag, discard marinade and grill chicken 4 to 5 inches from hot coals for about 13 to 15 minutes, depending on size of chicken breasts.

- Serve chicken as is or slice and place over mixed green salad. Serves 6.

Skillet Chicken Teriyaki Magic

5 - 6 boneless, skinless chicken breast halves
2 (10 ounce) cans golden mushroom soup
1 (1 ounce) package teriyaki seasoning mix
1 (16 ounce) package frozen stir-fry vegetables

- In large skillet, brown and cook chicken in a little oil. Remove chicken and set aside but keep warm.

- Add soup, 1 cup water, teriyaki seasoning and vegetables to skillet and heat to a boil.

- Return chicken to skillet. Reduce heat, cover and simmer for 10 minutes.

- Serve over hot cooked rice. Serves 5 to 6.

Sweet-and-Sour Chicken

6 - 8 boneless, skinless chicken breast halves
Oil
1 (1 ounce) package onion soup mix
1 (6 ounce) can frozen orange juice concentrate, thawed

- In skillet, brown chicken in a little oil. Place chicken in sprayed 9 x 13-inch baking dish.

- In small bowl, combine soup mix, orange juice and ⅔ cup water and mix well.

- Pour over chicken and bake uncovered at 350° for 45 to 50 minutes. Serves 6 to 8.

Chicken-Wild Rice Special

1 (6 ounce) package long grain-wild rice mix
4 boneless, skinless chicken breast halves
Vegetable oil
2 (10 ounce) cans French onion soup
2 green bell peppers, seeded, julienned

- In saucepan, cook rice according to package directions and keep warm.

- Brown chicken breasts on both sides in large skillet with a little oil over medium-high heat. Add soup, $\frac{3}{4}$ cup water and bell peppers. Reduce heat to medium-low, cover and cook for 15 minutes.

- To serve, place rice on serving platter with chicken breasts on top. Serve sauce in gravy boat to spoon over chicken and rice. Serves 4.

Sweet 'n Hot Chicken

$\frac{2}{3}$ cup orange marmalade
2 tablespoons chili powder
8 chicken drumsticks
1 cup prepared dry, seasoned breadcrumbs

- Preheat oven to 400°. In shallow bowl, combine and mix marmalade, chili powder and $\frac{1}{2}$ teaspoon salt.

- Place breadcrumbs in separate shallow bowl, dip and roll drumsticks in crumbs.

- Place in large, sprayed baking sheet and arrange so drumsticks do not touch. Bake for 25 to 30 minutes. Serves 4.

Parmesan Dip Sticks

1½ pounds chicken tenders, cut into strips
⅓ cup grated parmesan cheese
1 (9 ounce) box extra crispy, seasoned coating mix
1 (16 ounce) jar barbecue sauce

- Rinse chicken tenders and shake off excess water. (Cut large pieces in half lengthwise.)

- Preheat oven to 400°. Place cheese and coating mix in shaker bag. Add few tenders at a time and shake until they coat well. Repeat with remaining tenders.

- Place on large, sprayed baking sheet with sides. Discard remaining coating mixture. Bake for 14 minutes or until chicken is well done. Serve barbecue sauce for dipping. Serves 8.

Cajun Chicken Strips

⅓ cup flour
1 tablespoon Cajun seasoning mix
1 teaspoon poultry seasoning
1 teaspoon paprika
1½ pounds chicken tenders

- In large, resealable plastic bag, combine flour, Cajun and poultry seasonings and paprika. Shake to mix well.

- Add chicken in batches and shake to coat well. In large skillet with a little oil, cook chicken few pieces at a time for 10 minutes. Serves 6.

Chicken Fajitas Express

1 red bell pepper, seeded, julienned
1 green bell pepper, seeded, julienned
¼ cup oil
1 pound boneless, skinless chicken breasts, cut into thin strips
1 (1 ounce) package onion soup mix

• Saute pepper in oil for 2 minutes, add chicken and cook 5 to 6 minutes or until chicken is light brown.

• Stir in soup mix plus ½ cup water. Simmer 3 minutes or until chicken is no longer pink.

• Heat package of flour tortillas and roll chicken-pepper mixture in tortillas. Serves 6.

Honey-Mustard Chicken Tenders

1 pound boneless, skinless chicken tenders
3½ tablespoons honey mustard
1⅓ cups French-fried onions, crushed

• Coat chicken with mustard and roll in crushed onions.

• Place on sprayed 9 x 13-inch baking pan and bake at 400° for 15 minutes or until chicken is done. Serves 4 to 8.

The Central Valley of California from Sacramento to Bakersfield is, acre for acre, the richest agricultural area in the world.

Quick Chicken Quesadillas

2 cups finely diced, cooked chicken or turkey
1 (10 ounce) can southwest-style pepper jack soup
8 (8-inch) flour tortillas, warmed
1 (16 ounce) jar chunky salsa

- Preheat oven to 425°. In saucepan, combine chicken and soup. Heat well and spoon $\frac{1}{3}$ cup chicken mixture on half of each tortilla. Leave $\frac{1}{2}$-inch edge. Moisten edge with water and fold to seal.

- Place quesadillas on 2 large baking sheets and bake for 5 to 8 minutes. Cut in wedges to serve. Serves 6 to 8.

Surprise Sauce for Chicken

This recipe sounds awful, but tastes delicious. It will surprise you.

1 (15 ounce) can whole berry cranberry sauce
1 (1 ounce) package onion soup mix
1 (8 ounce) bottle French salad dressing
6 - 8 boneless, skinless chicken breast halves

- In bowl, combine cranberry sauce, soup mix and salad dressing and mix well.

- Cover and refrigerate until ready to use.

- Place chicken breasts in baking dish and pour cranberry sauce evenly over chicken.

- Cover and marinate overnight in refrigerator. Next day, bake at 350° for 1 hour or until tender. Serves 6 to 8.

Sew 'n Sew's Chicken Wings

1 cup flour
2 teaspoons paprika
22 - 24 chicken wings

- Preheat oven to 325°.

- In large, resealable plastic bag, combine flour, 2 teaspoons salt, 1 teaspoon pepper and paprika. Toss chicken wings in flour mixture and coat well.

- Place in large, sprayed baking dish. Bake uncovered for 30 minutes.

Sauce:

$\frac{1}{3}$ cup honey
$\frac{1}{4}$ cup orange juice concentrate, thawed
$\frac{1}{2}$ teaspoon dried ginger
1 tablespoon dried parsley

- In bowl, combine honey, orange juice and ginger and brush generously over chicken wings.

- Reduce heat to 300° and bake another 35 minutes. Baste with sauce.

- To serve, sprinkle parsley over chicken wings. Serves 8 to 12.

10 Good Reasons to Have Meals at Home are included in this cookbook. Here's one of them.

6. Family meals help children learn financial responsibility. They see how a family must live within their means and provide nutritional meals to avoid health problems like diabetes and heart disease. Eating out is more expensive, the food has more calories and the family time is lost. Eating out is for special occasions.

Beef Tips and Noodles

1½ pounds stew meat, fat trimmed
2 (10 ounce) cans cream of onion soup, diluted
1 (8 ounce) package noodles

- In greased skillet, brown stew meat and add soup diluted with 1 cup water.

- Allow meat to simmer for 3 hours. Stir occasionally.

- In separate saucepan, cook noodles according to package directions.

- Serve over noodles. Serves 6 to 8.

Fiesta Beef and Pasta Shells

1 (16 ounce) package medium shell pasta
1½ pounds lean ground beef
1 (16 ounce) jar hot, chunky salsa
1 (12 ounce) package cubed Velveeta® cheese

- Preheat oven to 350°. Cook pasta according to package directions, drain and set aside. In large skillet, brown ground beef until it cooks well done and drain.

- In microwave-safe dish, combine salsa and cheese. Microwave 3 to 4 minutes or until cheese melts. Combine with beef in skillet, add pasta and stir well. Transfer to sprayed 9 x 13-inch baking pan and bake uncovered for 30 minutes.

- If you desire, sprinkle crushed chips over top of casserole during last 10 minutes of cooking time. Serves 8.

Heritage Pinto Bean Pie

1 pound lean ground beef
1 onion, chopped
2 (15 ounce) cans pinto beans with liquid, divided
1 (10 ounce) can diced tomatoes and green chilies with liquid
1 (3 ounce) can French-fried onions

- In skillet, brown beef and onion and drain well.

- In 2-quart casserole dish, layer 1 can beans, beef-onion mixture and ½ can tomatoes and green chilies. Repeat layer.

- Top with onions and bake uncovered at 350° for 30 minutes. Serves 6 to 8.

Saucy Chili

2 pounds ground beef or ground round
2 (1 ounce) packets chili seasoning
2 (32 ounce) jars spaghetti sauce with chunky tomatoes, onions, peppers

- In heavy skillet, brown meat, drain and stir in chili seasoning.

- Add sauce and 1 cup water to skillet mixture and mix well. Simmer for 30 minutes. Serves 6.

TIP: If you have to have beans in your chili, add 1 or 2 cans pinto beans and heat for 20 minutes longer.

If you know beans about chili, you know chili has no beans.

-Jerry Jeff Walker

Savory Steak Supper

1½ pounds boneless round steak, cut in thin slices
1 (10 ounce) can cream of mushroom soup
1 (1 ounce) package dry onion soup mix
⅔ cup milk
⅔ cup sour cream
1 (10 ounce) package medium-size noodles

- In large skillet with a little oil, brown steak pieces. Stir in soup, milk, soup mix and heavy sprinkling black pepper and mix well. On high heat, bring mixture to boil. Reduce heat, cover and simmer for 20 minutes.

- Cook noodles according to packing directions. Just before serving, stir sour cream into hot steak mixture and serve over noodles. Serves 8.

Unstuffed Cabbage with Beef

1½ pounds lean ground beef
1 large onion, chopped
½ head cabbage, coarsely chopped
1 (8 ounce) can tomato sauce
2 tablespoons lemon juice
½ teaspoon cinnamon

- In large skillet, brown beef and sprinkle with salt and pepper. Stir well to cook evenly. Cover and simmer on low for 10 minutes.

- Stir in onion, cabbage, tomato sauce, lemon juice and cinnamon. Heat to boil and reduce heat. Cover and simmer for 10 minutes. Serves 8.

TIP: To chop cabbage, use only outer, green leaves and discard white middle.

Skillet Steak, Potatoes and Gravy

7 - 8 medium red, new potatoes, cut into 4 pieces
1½ pounds boneless beef sirloin steak, thinly sliced
1 onion, chopped
1 bell pepper, julienned
2 teaspoons minced garlic
⅓ cup cornstarch
1 (14 ounce) can beef broth

- In saucepan, cook potatoes in a little water over high heat for 10 to 15 minutes or until tender. Drain.

- In large skillet with a little oil, brown sirloin slices until beef is no longer pink. Place beef on platter and keep warm. In same skillet, saute onion, bell pepper and garlic using another tablespoon of oil.

- Return beef to skillet and add potatoes. Combine cornstarch and beef broth and pour into skillet. Bring mixture to boil, stir and cook for 2 minutes or until mixture is thick. Serves 8.

Make-Believe Filet Mignon

2 pounds ground round steak
1 (1 ounce) package dry onion soup mix
6 bacon slices

- In bowl, combine steak and soup mix.

- Shape into 6 thick patties and wrap slice of bacon around each.

- Secure with wooden picks, place in 9 x 13-inch dish and bake at 450° for 15 to 20 minutes or broil on each side. Serves 6.

Hamburger Steak with Onion Sauce

1½ pounds lean ground beef
½ cup dry, seasoned breadcrumbs
1 large egg
1 tablespoon Worcestershire sauce

- Preheat broiler and spray foil-lined broiler pan with nonstick cooking spray. In large bowl, combine ground beef, breadcrumbs, egg and Worcestershire sauce. Shape into 6 patties and place on broiler pan.

- Broil, turning once, about 10 minutes or until well done.

Onion Sauce:

2 onions, thinly sliced
2 tablespoons (¼ stick) butter
1 tablespoon flour
1 (10 ounce) can French onion soup

- In skillet, saute onions in butter. Stir in flour and mix well. Pour in onion soup and heat. Stir constantly until soup is thick.

- To serve, spoon onion sauce over beef patties. Serves 8.

10 Good Reasons to Have Meals at Home are included in this cookbook. Here's one of them.

7. Harvard University's "Archives of Family Medicine" published in March 2000 stated that eating meals at home during the week is directly associated with better nutrition in children. They got more nutrients such calcium, iron, fiber, vitamin B6, vitamin C, vitamin E and consumed less fat eating at home than eating out.

Stir-It-Up Beef Stew

1 pound boneless, beef sirloin steak, cut into 1-inch cubes
1 (10 ounce) can tomato soup
1 (10 ounce) can French onion soup
1 (15 ounce) can Mexican stewed tomatoes
1 (16 ounce) package frozen mixed vegetables

- In soup pot with a little oil, brown steak and simmer for 5 minutes. Stir several times.

- Add soups, stewed tomatoes, mixed vegetables plus ½ cup water.

- Cover and cook over low to medium heat for 10 minutes or until vegetables are tender. Serves 8 to 10.

Delicious Meatloaf

1½ pounds lean ground beef
⅔ cup dry, Italian-seasoned breadcrumbs
1 egg, beaten
1 (10 ounce) can golden mushroom soup, divided
2 tablespoons (¼ stick) butter

- In bowl, mix beef, breadcrumbs, ½ mushroom soup and egg thoroughly and shape mixture firmly into 8 x 4-inch loaf. Bake at 350° for 45 minutes.

- In small saucepan, mix 2 tablespoons butter, remaining soup and ¼ cup water. Heat thoroughly. Serves 8 to 10.

Those who have been intoxicated with power... can never willingly abandon it.
                                    -Edmund Burke

Peppered Meatloaf

1¼ cups dry Italian-seasoned breadcrumbs
1 egg
1½ pounds lean ground beef
¾ (8 ounce) package shredded pepper jack cheese

• Preheat oven to 350°. In large bowl, combine breadcrumbs, egg and crumbled ground beef. Sprinkle with a little salt and pepper and mix well (mix it with your hands).

• Spoon half mixture into sprayed 8 x 4-inch loaf pan, press down and half way up sides of pan. Sprinkle half cheese over meat to within ½-inch of sides. Pat remaining beef mixture over cheese.

• Bake uncovered for 50 to 55 minutes. Sprinkle remaining cheese over top and let stand 10 to 15 minutes before slicing. Serves 8 to 10.

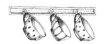

Signature Meatloaf with Gravy

1 (14 ounce) can seasoned beef broth with onion, divided
1½ pounds extra lean ground beef
⅔ cup dry, Italian-seasoned breadcrumbs
1 egg, beaten
1 tablespoon flour

• Preheat oven to 350°. In large bowl, combine ¼ cup broth, ground beef, breadcrumbs and egg and mix well. Shape firmly into 8 x 4-inch loaf pan and bake for 1 hour.

• In saucepan, combine remaining broth and flour to make gravy. Heat and stir constantly until mixture is thick. Serve over meatloaf. Serves 10.

Sassy Meatballs

1 (30 ounce) package frozen meatballs, thawed
1 (16 ounce) package frozen chopped onion and bell pepper
1 (15 ounce) can sliced carrots, drained
2 (10 ounce) jars sweet-and-sour sauce
1 tablespoon soy sauce
2 tablespoons minced garlic

- In large saucepan, combine all ingredients plus $\frac{1}{4}$ cup water. Cook on medium heat and stir constantly until mixture is hot. Stir in thawed meatballs and cook until meatballs are hot.

- Serve over hot, cooked rice. Serves 10 to 12.

Apricot-Spiced Brisket

1 (4 - 5 pound) trimmed brisket
1 (10 ounce) can shredded sauerkraut, drained
2 (12 ounce) jars apricot preserves
2 (8 ounce) bottles chili sauce

- Preheat oven to 375°. Place brisket, fat side up, in roasting pan and sprinkle with salt and pepper (add garlic powder if you desire).

- Combine sauerkraut, preserves and chili sauce. Pour over brisket, cover and cook for 1 hour. Reduce heat to 325° and cook for another 3 hours or until tender.

- Remove brisket from pan and set aside 20 minutes. Cut brisket into thin slices. Cut across grain for easier slicing.

- Remove sauce from pan and strain. Serve strained sauce with brisket. Serves 12 to 14.

Corned Beef Brisket Specialty

1 (3 - 4 pound) corned beef brisket
2 tablespoons prepared mustard
¼ cup packed brown sugar

• On top of stove over low heat, cook corned beef in pot of water for 2 hours 30 minutes.

• Remove beef from pot, place in 9 x 13-inch roasting or broiler pan. Poke holes in meat with fork.

• In bowl, mix mustard and brown sugar until creamy and paste forms.

• Spread mixture over entire brisket and bake at 350° for 1 hour 30 minutes or until tender. Serves 10 to 12.

Weaver's Brisket

1 (3 - 4 pound) brisket
1 (8 ounce) bottle chili sauce
1 (12 ounce) can cola soda
1 (1 ounce) package dry onion soup mix

• To prepare brisket, place 3 to 4-pound brisket in roasting pan with lid.

• Combine remaining ingredients in bowl and mix well to make 2½ cups sauce.

• Pour sauce over brisket, cover and bake at 325° for 3 to 5 hours or for 30 minutes per pound until tender.

• Pour off sauce and serve in gravy bowl with brisket. Serves 10 to 12.

TIP: Use regular soda, not diet, for this sauce. It is much better.

Party Roasted Brisket

1 (5 pound) beef brisket
1 (6 ounce) can frozen lemon juice concentrate
1 (1 ounce) package dry onion soup mix

- Trim off all visible fat from meat and place in 9 x 13-inch roasting pan.

- Make smooth paste by combining enough thawed lemon juice concentrate into soup mix. Spread paste over meat and cover tightly with foil or lid.

- Bake at 250° for 5 to 6 hours or until fork-tender. Serves 10 to 12.

Welcome Home Roast Beef

1 (3 pound) rump or chuck roast
1 (1 ounce) package dry onion soup mix
½ teaspoon of garlic powder

- Place beef roast on large sheet of foil.

- Sprinkle roast with 1 package soup mix and dash of garlic powder and seal foil.

- Place in large pan and bake at 325° for 1 hour 30 minutes or until tender (or bake at 200° for 8 to 9 hours, depending on size roast). Serves 8 to 10.

Make peace with your past so it won't ruin your present.

Sunday House Pot Roast

4 - 6 pound boneless rump roast
1 (1 ounce) package dry onion soup mix
Garlic powder
Seasoned pepper

- Preheat oven to 375°. Place roast in large roasting pan with 1½ to 2 cups water. Sprinkle soup mix, garlic powder and seasoned pepper over top.

- Cover and cook for 45 minutes. Reduce heat to 325° and cook another 3 hours.

Vegetables and Gravy:

4 medium potatoes, peeled, quartered
1 (16 ounce) package baby carrots
3 small onions, halved
1 (14 ounce) can beef broth, divided
⅓ cup cornstarch

- After roast cooks, add potatoes, carrots and onions. Return to 375° oven and cook another 35 to 45 minutes or until vegetables are tender. Remove roast to serving platter and set aside 20 to 30 minutes before slicing.

- In small bowl, combine ½ cup broth and cornstarch and stir well. Place roasting pan on high heat on top burner. Pour in broth-cornstarch mixture and remaining broth into pan and stir constantly until gravy thickens.

- Spoon vegetables around roast and serve in gravy boat. Serves 10 to 12.

There are nine distinct regional cuisines in the U.S.: Tex-Mex, Cajun-Creole, Southern, New England, Pennsylvania Dutch, Southwest, Pacific Rim, Heartland and Floribbean.

Yankee Pot Roast

1 (4 - 5 pound) beef pot roast
2 (10 ounce) cans French onion soup
6 potatoes, peeled, quartered

- Brown meat on all sides in iron skillet or Dutch oven.

- Add soup, cover and cook on low heat for 3 to 4 hours or until roast is fork-tender.

- Add potatoes after meat cooks for 2 hours and continue cooking until done. Serves 8.

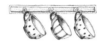

Incredibly Easy, Incredibly Good Ribs

1 slab beef short ribs
1 tablespoon seasoning salt
1 (8 ounce) bottle Italian salad dressing

- Spread coals evenly on grill, open bottom vent halfway and light coals.

- Place ribs, bone down, in bottom layer of foil and "paint" ribs with dressing.

- Sprinkle with seasoning and cover top with foil.

- When fire is out on coals, place wrapped ribs on grill and cover.

- Close top vent until only a light is visible and cook for 6 hours. Turn ribs every 2 hours. At hour 6, remove foil top and puncture bottom foil to drain. Serves 6 to 8.

TIP: If you want your ribs "wet", coat with barbecue sauce and cook 45 to 60 minutes more.

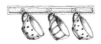

Apricot-Glazed Ham

1 (about 5 pounds) boneless ham half
1 (12 ounce) jar apricot preserves
2 tablespoons dijon-style mustard
¼ cup packed brown sugar

- Preheat oven to 350°. Cook ham according to package directions. Remove ham from oven 30 minutes prior to end of cooking time.

- In bowl, combine apricot preserves, mustard and brown sugar. Spoon and brush mixture over ham and return to oven for remaining cooking time. Baste occasionally.

- Slice ham and serve with remaining glaze. Serves 10 to 12.

Citrus-Spiced Ham

1 (3 - 4 pound) fully cooked ham
1 (12 ounce) jar orange marmalade
2 tablespoons lemon juice
¼ cup (½ stick) butter
½ teaspoon cinnamon

- Preheat oven to 325°. Place ham on sprayed baking pan and bake uncovered for 45 minutes.

- In skillet, combine orange marmalade, lemon juice, butter and cinnamon. Heat and stir well. Brush ¼ cup sauce mixture over ham and cook another 15 minutes.

- Warm sauce and serve with ham slices. Serves 10.

Designer's Ham Special

1 or 2 (16 ounce) center-cut ham slices

Fruit Topping:

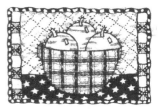

¼ cup (½ stick) butter
½ teaspoon cinnamon
½ cup packed brown sugar
1 (20 ounce) can apple pie filling
1 (15 ounce) can fruit cocktail, drained

- In large skillet, lightly brown ham on both sides and place on serving platter.

- In saucepan, combine butter, cinnamon, brown sugar, apple pie filling and fruit cocktail. Stir gently on medium heat until butter and sugar mix well with fruit.

- Spoon ⅓ cup fruit on individual slices of ham before serving. Serves 6 to 8.

Honey-Dijon Ham

1 (3 pound) boneless ham, cooked
½ cup honey
3 tablespoons dijon-style mustard
¼ cup packed brown sugar

- Preheat oven to 325°. Place ham on sprayed rack in shallow roasting pan. Bake for 50 minutes.

- In bowl, combine honey, mustard and brown sugar. Brush 3 tablespoons mixture over ham and continue to bake another 15 minutes.

- Heat remaining glaze and serve with ham. Serves 8.

Jiffy Ham Bake

1 (10 ounce) can cream of chicken soup
1 (8 ounce) package shredded Mexican 4-cheese blend, divided
1 (16 ounce) package frozen mixed vegetables, thawed
1 cup cooked instant rice
1 cup cooked ham, diced

- Preheat oven to 350°. In large saucepan, combine soup and half cheese and heat on LOW until cheese melts. Stir in vegetables and rice. Transfer mixture into sprayed 2-quart casserole dish.

- Bake uncovered for 25 minutes. Remove from oven, sprinkle remaining cheese and bake another 5 minutes. Serves 8.

TIP: This is a good recipe for leftover ham.

Peach-Glazed Ham

1 (3 pound) boneless ham, cooked
¾ cup packed brown sugar
2 tablespoons prepared mustard
½ cup peach preserves

- Preheat oven to 350°. Place ham on sprayed rack in shallow roasting pan. Pierce ham several times with fork.

- In bowl, combine brown sugar and mustard and mix well. Spread sugar-mustard mixture over ham and then spread with preserves.

- Cover with foil and bake for 1 hour. Baste occasionally, uncover and bake another 30 minutes. Serves 8.

Quick Potato-Ham Supper

4 - 5 cups new (red) potatoes with peels, cubed, cooked
3 cups cooked ham, diced
¾ cup mayonnaise
1 (8 ounce) package shredded Mexican 4-cheese blend

- In large skillet, combine cooked potatoes, ham, mayonnaise and salt and pepper.

- Heat on medium until hot. Stir in cheese and heat until cheese melts. Serves 10 to 12.

TIP: If you would like to "dress up" this supper, sprinkle 1 (3 ounce) can French-fried onions or a few chopped, fresh green onions.

Mac and Ham Supper

1 (7 ounce) box macaroni and cheese
2 cups cooked ham, chopped
1 (8 ounce) package frozen baby peas
½ cup sour cream
1½ cups dry, seasoned croutons, crushed

- Preheat oven to 350°. Prepare macaroni and cheese according to package directions. Add ham, peas and sour cream and mix well.

- Spoon into sprayed 9 x 13-inch baking dish and sprinkle crushed croutons on top.

- Bake for 20 minutes. Serves 8 to 10.

Tortellini-Ham Supper Bake

1 (16 ounce) package sun-dried tomato and oregano-filled tortellini
2 - 3 cups leftover cubed ham, warmed

Sauce:

$\frac{2}{3}$ cup extra virgin olive oil
2 heaping teaspoons prepared minced garlic
1 onion, finely chopped
1 zucchini, finely chopped
1 teaspoon dried minced parsley

- Cook tortellini according to package directions, drain and keep warm.

- In skillet with olive oil, saute garlic, onion and zucchini. Spoon into saucepan with cooked tortellini and stir in parsley. Mix well and transfer to serving dish.

- Place cubed ham over top and serve immediately. Serves 10.

Grandpa's Ham and Red-Eye Gravy

$2\frac{1}{2}$ cups hot, strong-brewed coffee
$\frac{1}{3}$ cup packed brown sugar
1 pound country ham, thick-sliced, center-cut

- In bowl, combine coffee and sugar. In large skillet, cook ham over medium heat 5 minutes on each side. Remove ham to serving plate and keep warm.

- Add coffee-sugar mixture to skillet and bring to boil. Stir occasionally to loosen particles from bottom of skillet.

- Continue cooking until mixture reduces by half. Serve with ham. Serves 6.

Hawaiian Ham Steaks

1 (8½ ounce) can sliced pineapple with juice
2 tablespoons packed brown sugar
1 pound center-cut ham steak

- Pour ½-inch juice into skillet and stir in brown sugar.

- Make slashes in fat around ham to keep it from curling. Place ham in skillet with juice mixture and top with pineapple slices.

- Cook on medium low heat and turn twice. Cook until sauce becomes thick and serve with pineapple slice on each serving. Serves 4 to 6.

Easter Holiday Ham

1 (5 - 6 pound) cooked ham
1 (6 ounce) jar dijon-style mustard
1 (16 ounce) jar apricot jam
½ cup dry sherry

- Preheat oven to 300°. Place ham in baking dish and cover with foil. Bake for 1 hour.

- In bowl, combine mustard, jam and dry sherry and mix well.

- Remove foil from ham and spoon about ¾ cup mustard mixture over ham and continue cooking for 1 hour. Baste several times.

- Heat remaining glaze and serve with ham. Serves 10 to 12.

I never did give them hell. I just told the truth and they thought it was hell.
-Harry S Truman

Grilled, Marinated Pork Tenderloin

2 (1-pound) pork tenderloins
¾ cup roasted garlic-herb marinade
Black pepper

- Butterfly pork lengthwise (be careful not to cut all the way through) and press open to flatten. Place tenderloins in large, resealable plastic bag and pour in marinade mix. Seal bag and turn over several times to coat well. Marinade for 20 to 30 minutes.

- Grill 5 inches from hot coals for 8 minutes. Turn tenderloin over, brush on additional marinade and grill for another 6 minutes. Serves 8.

TIP: Pork tenderloin dries out quickly so be careful not to overcook.

Teriyaki Tenderloin

¾ cup soy sauce
½ cup sugar
3 tablespoons ketchup
2 (1 pound) pork tenderloins

- Combine soy sauce, sugar and ketchup in resealable plastic bag. Add pork tenderloin, to bag and turn several times to coat pork. Refrigerate for 8 hours or overnight.

- Preheat oven to 400°. Drain and discard marinade and place pork tenderloin in sprayed 9 x 13-inch baking dish.

- Cover and bake for 40 minutes. Uncover and cook for another 5 to 10 minutes to brown tenderloin. To serve, let stand about 5 minutes and slice. Serves 10 to 12.

Pork Tenderloin with Red Pepper Sauce

2 (1 pound each) pork tenderloins
1 teaspoon garlic salt
1 teaspoon black pepper

- Preheat oven to 350°. Sprinkle tenderloins with garlic salt and pepper and bake uncovered for 50 minutes.

- When ready to serve, slice tenderloins.

Red Pepper Sauce:

1 onion, chopped
1 (10 ounce) jar roasted red peppers, rinsed
1 (8 ounce) carton sour cream
1 (1 ounce) packet ranch-style dressing mix

- In skillet, saute onion in a little oil. Stir in red peppers and heat thoroughly.

- Remove skillet from heat and stir in sour cream and dressing. Transfer to food processor and puree until smooth. Serve warm over sliced tenderloins. Serves 8 to 10

Dijon Pork Chops

6 loin pork chops
½ cup packed brown sugar
2 teaspoons dijon-style mustard

- Arrange pork chops in sprayed 9 x 13-inch baking dish. Combine sugar and mustard in small dish and mix well.

- Spread mixture on top of chops and bake covered at 350° for 45 minutes. Uncover and bake about 10 minutes longer or until brown. Serves 6.

Grilled Honey-Maple Pork Chops

¼ cup honey
¼ cup maple-flavored syrup
¼ teaspoon allspice
6 (6 ounce, ¾-inch thick) pork loin chops

- In bowl, combine honey, syrup and allspice and mix well. Sprinkle pork chops with a little salt and pepper.

- When ready to grill, brush pork chops heavily with honey mixture. Place on grill, cover and cook 12 to 14 minutes.

- Turn once and brush occasionally with honey mixture. Serves 6.

Honey-Mustard Pork Chops

6 (1-inch thick) boneless pork chops
¾ cup dijon-style mustard
½ cup honey
2 teaspoons dried thyme leaves

- Sprinkle salt and pepper over pork chops and brown in skillet on both sides.

- While pork chops brown, combine mustard, honey and thyme leaves in saucepan. Heat and spoon mixtures over pork chops before serving. Serves 6.

An excellent health tip: Take a 10 to 30-Minute Walk Everyday and Smile While Doing It.

Onion-Smothered Pork Chops

1 tablespoon oil
6 (½-inch) thick pork chops
1 onion, chopped
2 tablespoons (¼ stick) butter
1 (10 ounce) can cream of onion soup

- In skillet, brown pork chops in oil and simmer for about 10 minutes.

- In same skillet, add butter and saute chopped onion. (Pan juices from pork chops are brown so onions will turn brown from juices in skillet.)

- Add onion soup and ½ cup water. Stir well to create light brown color.

- Pour onion-soup mixture over pork chops, cover and bake at 325° for 40 minutes. Serves 6.

TIP: This is great served with Uncle Ben's brown rice.

Presto Pork Supper

1 (1 pound) pork tenderloin, cut in ¼-inch strips
1 bunch fresh broccoli florets (no stems)
1 red bell pepper, seeded, julienned
2 (3 ounce) packages pork ramen noodles
1 tablespoon marinade for chicken

- In large skillet with a little oil, combine pork strips, broccoli and bell pepper. Cook 10 minutes until pork is no longer pink.

- Add 1½ cups water, noodles plus seasoning packets and marinade for chicken. Stir well and bring to boil. Reduce heat, cover and cook 3 to 4 minutes or until noodles are al dente. Serves 10.

Cranberry-Glazed Pork Roast

1 (6 pound) pork shoulder roast
1 (16 ounce) can whole cranberry sauce
¼ cup packed brown sugar

- Place pork on rack in roasting pan and roast at 325° for
  3 hours or until fork-tender. (If using meat thermometer,
  it should register 185°.)

- Remove roast, pour off drippings and trim skin and fat.
  Return meat to pan.

- In bowl, mash cranberry sauce with fork, stir in brown sugar
  and mix well. Cut deep gashes in meat and brush generously
  with cranberry sauce mixture.

- Bake at 350° for about 30 minutes and brush often
  with glaze. Serves 10 to 12.

Mustard-Glazed Pork Roast

1 (3 - 4 pound) pork loin
1 cup light corn syrup
½ cup packed brown sugar
¼ cup prepared mustard

- Preheat oven to 350°. Place pork in roasting pan and bake
  for 30 minutes per pound.

- In bowl, combine corn syrup, sugar and mustard. Brush ham
  with glaze mixture several times during last 30 minutes
  of cooking.

- Glaze can also be used with baked ham. Serves 10 to 12.

Skillet Spareribs

2 - 3 pounds bone-in spareribs
2 (12 ounce) cans cola drink
1 (12 ounce) bottle chili sauce
2 tablespoons packed brown sugar
2 tablespoons cornstarch

- In large heavy skillet, brown spareribs and drain well. Stir in cola, chili sauce and brown sugar and heat to boil. Reduce heat, cover and simmer for 1 hour 30 minutes or until tender. Remove ribs and keep warm.

- In small bowl, combine cornstarch and $\frac{1}{4}$ cup water. Stir sauce into skillet and bring mixture to boil. Stir constantly and cook until sauce is thick. Serve over spareribs. Serves 8.

The pioneer era began in the 1800's when many families left their homes to explore new opportunities in the West.

A "Friendship Quilt" with blocks signed by family and friends were often given as a loving, parting remembrance. Often it was the last time they would see each other and these quilts were treasured gifts.

The "Patchwork Quilt" is a distinctive American quilt form that originated as settlers moved away from the textile mills and availability of fabric. The scarcity of fabric led quilters to use and adapt patterns that would allow frugal use of scraps.

French Fish Fillets

1 pound fish fillets
¼ cup French salad dressing
½ cup cracker crumbs

- Dip fillets in dressing and roll in crumbs. Coat well.

- Place in baking dish and bake at 350° for about 10 minutes.

- Turn fish and cook 10 minutes longer or until fish is lightly brown. Serves 4 to 6.

Fisherman's Catch

2 eggs, well beaten
Lemon pepper
2 cups crushed crackers
6 (2 - 3 ounce) cod fillets (or favorite fish)

- In shallow bowl, add eggs, tablespoon water and generous amount lemon pepper.

- Place crushed crackers in separate bowl and add a little more lemon pepper.

- Dip fillets in egg mixture and then in cracker crumbs. Press down to coat well.

- On medium to high heat, pour ¼-inch of oil in large skillet. Fry fillets 4 to 5 minutes on each side. Serves 6.

Use fish from only the best schools.

Savory Tuna Steaks

⅓ cup light soy sauce
1 tablespoon sugar
2 teaspoons prepared minced garlic
4 (6 ounce) tuna steaks

- In bowl, combine soy sauce, sugar and garlic. Place one side of tuna in soy sauce mixture and turn to coat.

- Broil steaks about 5 inches from heat for 10 to 12 minutes and turn once. Brush frequently with remaining soy sauce mixture. Serves 4.

Easy Tuna Casserole

2 cups crushed potato chips
2 (6 ounce) cans tuna fish, drained
2 (10 ounce) cans cream of mushroom soup

- Place 1 layer of crushed potato chips in sprayed casserole dish and top with layer of tuna. Repeat layers and pour mushroom soup over tuna.

- Bake at 350° for 25 minutes. Serves 8.

Creamy Tuna Treat

1 (8 ounce) package frozen mixed vegetables, thawed
1 (8 ounce) can green peas or whole kernel corn, drained
1 (12 ounce) can tuna, drained
1 (10 ounce) can cream of chicken soup

- In large saucepan, combine mixed vegetables, peas or corn, tuna and soup.

- Cook on low to medium heat and stir twice about 5 minutes.

- Serve over hot, cooked rice or noodles. Serves 8.

Me-O, Mi-O Flounder Italiano

4 - 6 frozen flounder fillets
1½ cups spaghetti sauce
½ cup shredded mozzarella cheese

- Place fillets in sprayed 9 x 13-inch pan and pour spaghetti sauce over fillets.

- Bake uncovered at 350° for about 30 minutes and sprinkle with cheese. Bake 5 minutes longer or until cheese melts. Serves 4 to 6.

So Simple Marinated Salmon

1 (8 ounce) bottle raspberry vinaigrette salad dressing
4 - 6 (4-ounce) salmon fillets

- Place ½ bottle dressing in resealable plastic bag. Add salmon fillets and turn several times to coat well.

- Broil 2 to 4 inches from broiler for 10 to 14 minutes or until salmon flakes easily with a fork. Serves 4 to 6.

Pecan-Baked Salmon

4 - 5 (4-ounce) salmon fillets
⅔ cup finely chopped pecans
½ cup dry, seasoned breadcrumbs
¼ cup grated parmesan cheese

- Preheat oven to 400°. Place salmon, skin side down, on sprayed 9 x 13-inch baking pan. Brush a little olive oil over fillets.

- In bowl, combine pecans, breadcrumbs and cheese. Sprinkle pecan-cheese mixture over each fillet and bake for 10 to 15 minutes or until fish flakes easily with a fork. Serves 4 to 5.

Orange Roughy Ready

4 - 6 orange roughy fillets
½ cup orange marmalade
3 tablespoons butter
1 tablespoon dijon-style mustard

- Place orange roughy fillets in shallow baking pan and broil for 5 to 6 minutes.

- In saucepan, combine marmalade, butter and mustard. Mix well and heat until butter melts. Spoon mixture over fillets and broil an additional 5 minutes.

- Before serving, brush more of marmalade mixture over fillets. Serves 4 to 6.

Shrimp and Veggies over Rice

¼ cup (½ stick) butter
¾ cup chopped celery
¾ cup chopped bell pepper
1 pound fresh shrimp, deveined
1 (10 ounce) can cream of chicken soup
½ teaspoon cayenne pepper or paprika

- In skillet, melt butter and saute celery and bell pepper. Add shrimp and cook on medium heat for 4 to 5 minutes.

- Add soup, cayenne pepper or paprika and ½ cup water and heat to boil. Remove from heat and serve over hot, cooked rice. Serves 6 to 8.

All power tends to corrupt; absolute power corrupts absolutely.

-Lord Acton

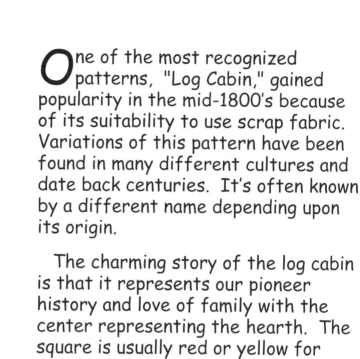

One of the most recognized patterns, "Log Cabin," gained popularity in the mid-1800's because of its suitability to use scrap fabric. Variations of this pattern have been found in many different cultures and date back centuries. It's often known by a different name depending upon its origin.

The charming story of the log cabin is that it represents our pioneer history and love of family with the center representing the hearth. The square is usually red or yellow for warmth or heart of the home. The narrow fabric strips sewn around the center square represent the logs. The colors alternate between light and dark for contrast, and so the story goes, to represent the joy and sadness experienced in the home.

Blue-Ribbon Slow-Cooker Recipes

Time and Tide wait for no man,
but Time always stands still for
a woman of thirty.
-Robert Frost

Broccoli Dip

¾ cup (1½ sticks) butter
2 cups thinly sliced celery
1 onion, finely chopped
3 tablespoons flour
1 (10 ounce) can cream of chicken soup
1 (10 ounce) box chopped broccoli, thawed
1 (5 ounce) garlic cheese roll, cut in chunks

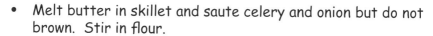

- Melt butter in skillet and saute celery and onion but do not brown. Stir in flour.

- Spoon into small slow cooker and stir in remaining ingredients and mix well.

- Cover and cook on LOW for 2 to 3 hours. Stir several times. Serve with wheat crackers or corn chips. Yields 1 quart.

Yummy Crab-Artichoke Spread

1 (6 ounce) can crabmeat, drained
½ cup grated parmesan cheese
1 bunch fresh green onion, sliced
1½ tablespoons lemon juice
1 (15 ounce) can artichoke hearts, drained, finely chopped
1 (8 ounce) package cream cheese, cubed

- In small slow cooker sprayed with vegetable cooking spray, combine all ingredients and stir well.

- Cover and cook on LOW for 1 hour to 1 hour 30 minutes. Stir until cream cheese mixes well.

- Serve on toasted bagel chips. Yields 2 cups.

Speedy Chicken-Enchilada Dip

2 pounds boneless, skinless chicken thighs, cubed
1 (10 ounce) can enchilada sauce
1 (7 ounce) can chopped green chilies, drained
1 small onion, finely chopped
1 large red bell pepper, finely chopped
2 (8 ounce) packages cream cheese, cubed
1 (16 ounce) package shredded American cheese

- In 4 to 5-quart slow cooker sprayed with vegetable cooking spray, place chicken thighs, enchilada sauce, green chilies, onion and bell pepper.

- Cover and cook on LOW 4 to 6 hours.

- Stir in cream cheese and American cheese and cook another 30 minutes. Stir several times during cooking. Serve with tortilla chips. Yields 2 quarts.

Pep, Pep Pepperoni Dip

1 (6 ounce) package pepperoni
1 bunch fresh green onion, thinly sliced
½ red bell pepper, finely chopped
1 medium tomato, finely chopped
1 (14 ounce) jar pizza sauce
1½ cups shredded mozzarella cheese
1 (8 ounce) package cream cheese, cubed

- Chop pepperoni into very small pieces and place in small slow cooker.

- Add green onion, bell pepper, tomato and pizza sauce and stir well.

- Cover and cook on LOW for 2 hours 30 minutes to 3 hours 30 minutes.

- Stir in mozzarella and cream cheese until cheeses melt. Serve with wheat crackers or tortilla chips. Yields 3 cups.

He-Man Hamburger Dip

Men love this meaty, spicy dip!

2 pounds lean ground beef
2 tablespoons dry minced onion
1½ teaspoons dried oregano leaves
1 tablespoon chili powder
2 teaspoons sugar
1 (10 ounce) can tomatoes and green chilies
½ cup chili sauce
1 (32 ounce) box Mexican Velveeta® cheese. cubed

- In large skillet, brown ground beef and drain. Transfer to 4 or 5-quart slow cooker sprayed with vegetable spray.

- Add remaining ingredients plus ½ to 1 cup water and stir well.

- Cover and cook on LOW for 1 hour 30 minutes to 2 hours. Stir once or twice during cooking time. Add a little salt if desired.

- Serve hot with chips or spread on crackers. Yields 2 quarts.

"Log Cabin" blocks can be set or sewn in many different combinations to create various optical illusions. Some of the best known and named for our pioneer heritage are: "Straight Furrow", "Barn Raising", "Sunshine and Shadow", "Windmill Blades", "Zig-Zag," and "Streaks of Lighting."

Delicious Broccoli-Cheese Soup

1 (16 ounce) package frozen chopped broccoli, thawed
1 (12 ounce) package cubed Velveeta® cheese
1 (1 ounce) package white sauce mix
1 (1 ounce) package vegetable soup mix
1 (12 ounce) can evaporated milk
1 (14 ounce) can chicken broth

- In large slow cooker sprayed with vegetable cooking spray, combine all ingredients plus 2 cups water. Stir well.

- Cover and cook on LOW for 6 to 7 hours or on HIGH for 3 hours 30 minutes to 4 hours. Stir about 1 hour before serving time. Serves 8.

Southern Vegetable Soup

1½ cups dry black-eyed peas
2 - 3 cups cooked, cubed ham
1 (15 ounce) can whole kernel corn
1 (10 ounce) package frozen cut okra, thawed
1 onion, chopped
1 large potato, cut into small cubes
2 teaspoons Cajun seasoning
1 (14 ounce) can chicken broth
2 (15 ounce) cans Mexican stewed tomatoes

- Rinse peas and drain. In large saucepan, combine peas and 5 cups water. Bring to boil, reduce heat and simmer for about 10 minutes. Drain.

- In 5 or 6-quart slow cooker, combine peas, ham, corn, okra, onion, potato, seasoning, broth and 2 cups water. Cover and cook on LOW for 6 to 8 hours.

- Add stewed tomatoes and continue cooking for 1 more hour. Serves 8.

Creamy Vegetable Soup

3 (14 ounce) cans chicken broth
¼ cup (½ stick) butter, melted
1 (16 ounce) package frozen mixed vegetables
1 onion, chopped
3 ribs celery, sliced
1 teaspoon ground cumin
3 zucchini, coarsely chopped
2 cups fresh, chopped broccoli
1 cup half-and-half cream

- In large slow cooker, combine broth, butter, mixed vegetables, onion, celery, cumin, and 1 teaspoon each of salt and pepper and stir well.

- Cover and cook on LOW for 6 to 7 hours or on HIGH for 3 to 4 hours.

- Stir in zucchini and broccoli. If not using HIGH temperature, turn heat to HIGH and cook for another 30 minutes to 1 hour or until broccoli is tender-crisp.

- Turn off heat and stir in cream. Let stand about 10 minutes before serving. Serves 8.

There can be no liberty for a community that lacks the means by which to detect lies.
–Walter Lippman

Rainy Day Meatball-Vegetable Soup

1 (32 ounce) package frozen meatballs
2 (15 ounce) cans stewed tomatoes
3 large potatoes, peeled, diced
4 carrots, peeled, sliced
2 medium onions, chopped
2 (14 ounce) cans beef broth
2 tablespoons cornstarch

- In sprayed 6-quart slow cooker, combine all ingredients except cornstarch. Add a little salt and pepper and 1 cup water. Cover and cook on LOW for 5 to 6 hours.

- Turn heat to HIGH and combine cornstarch with $\frac{1}{4}$ cup water. Pour into cooker and cook another 10 or 15 minutes or until slightly thick. Serves 8.

Italian Vegetable Stew

$1\frac{1}{2}$ - 2 pounds Italian sausage
2 (16 ounce) packages frozen vegetables
2 (15 ounce) cans Italian stewed tomatoes
1 (14 ounce) can beef broth
1 teaspoon Italian herb seasoning
$\frac{1}{2}$ cup pasta shells

- In skillet, cook sausage about 5 minutes or until brown. Drain.

- In 5 to 6-quart slow cooker, combine sausage with remaining ingredients and mix well. Cover and cook on LOW for 3 to 5 hours. Serves 8.

Admiral's Navy Bean Soup

8 slices thick-cut bacon, divided
1 carrot, sliced
3 (15 ounce) cans navy beans with liquid
3 ribs celery, chopped
1 onion, chopped
2 (15 ounce) cans chicken broth
1 teaspoon Italian herb seasoning
1 (10 ounce) can cream of chicken soup

- In skillet, cook, drain and crumble bacon. Set aside about 2 crumbled slices for garnish.

- Cut carrot in half lengthwise and slice.

- In 5 or 6-quart slow cooker, combine remaining ingredients except chicken soup. Add 1 cup water and most of crumbled bacon. Stir to mix.

- Cover and cook on LOW for 5 to 6 hours.

- Ladle 2 cups soup mixture into food processor or blender and process until smooth. Return to cooker, add cream of chicken soup and stir to mix.

- Turn heat to HIGH and cook another 10 to 15 minutes. Serves 6 to 8.

The "Log Cabin" block can also be associated with President Lincoln's Log Cabin Campaign. After the Civil War, it was sometimes given the name" Abe Lincoln's Log Cabin" in honor of the log cabin president.

Spicy Chicken-Tortilla Soup

3 large boneless, skinless chicken breast halves, cubed
1 (10 ounce) package frozen whole kernel corn, thawed
1 onion, chopped
3 (14 ounce) cans chicken broth
1 (6 ounce) can tomato paste
2 (10 ounce) cans tomatoes and green chilies
2 teaspoons ground cumin
1 teaspoon chili powder
1 teaspoon seasoned salt
1 teaspoon minced garlic
6 corn tortillas

- In large slow cooker, combine all ingredients except tortillas and mix well.

- Cover and cook on LOW for 5 to 7 hours or on HIGH for 3 to 3 hours 30 minutes.

- While soup is cooking, cut tortillas into ¼-inch strips and place on baking sheet.

- Bake at 375° for about 5 minutes or until crisp.

- Serve baked tortilla strips with soup. Serves 8.

I cldnuot blviee that I cluod aulaclty uesdnatnrd waht I was rdanieg. The phaonmneal pweor of the hmuan mnid. Aoccdrnig to rsceearch at Cmabrigde Uinervtisy, it deosn't mttaer in waht odrer the ltteers in a wrod are, the olny iprmoatnt tnhig is taht the frist and lsat ltteer be in the rghit pclae.

Fiesta Taco Soup

2 pounds lean ground beef
2 (15 ounce) cans ranch-style beans with liquid
1 (15 ounce) can whole kernel corn, drained
2 (15 ounce) cans stewed tomatoes
1 (10 ounce) can tomatoes and green chilies
1 (1 ounce) package ranch-style dressing mix
1 (1 ounce) package taco seasoning

- In large skillet, brown ground beef, drain and transfer to slow cooker.

- Add remaining ingredients and stir well.

- Cover and cook on LOW for 8 to 10 hours. Serves 8.

TIP: When serving, you might want to sprinkle shredded cheddar cheese over each serving.

Country Corn-Ham Chowder

1 (14 ounce) can chicken broth
1 cup whole milk
1 (10 ounce) can cream of celery soup
1 (15 ounce) can cream-style corn
1 (15 ounce) can whole kernel corn
½ cup dry potato flakes
1 onion, chopped
2 - 3 cups chopped, (leftover) cooked ham

- In 6-quart slow cooker, combine all ingredients and mix well.

- Cover and cook on LOW for 4 to 5 hours.

- When ready to serve, season with salt and black pepper. Serves 6 to 8.

Ham-Vegetable Chowder

Great recipe for leftover ham

1 medium potato
2 (10 ounce) cans cream of celery soup
1 (14 ounce) can chicken broth
3 cups finely diced ham
1 (15 ounce) can whole kernel corn
2 carrots, sliced
1 onion, coarsely chopped
1 teaspoon dried basil
1 teaspoon seasoned salt
1 teaspoon white pepper
1 (10 ounce) package frozen broccoli florets

- Cut potato into 1-inch pieces. Combine all ingredients except broccoli in large slow cooker. Cover and cook on LOW for 5 to 6 hours.

- Add broccoli to cooker and cook 1 hour more. Serves 8.

Chicken-Tortellini Stew

1 (9 ounce) package cheese-filled tortellini
2 small to medium yellow squash, halved, sliced
1 red bell pepper, coarsely chopped
1 onion, chopped
2 (14 ounce) cans chicken broth
1 teaspoon dried rosemary
½ teaspoon dried basil
2 cups cooked, chopped chicken

- Place tortellini, squash, bell pepper and onion in slow cooker.

- Stir in broth, rosemary, basil and chicken.

- Cover and cook on LOW for 2 to 4 hours or until tortellini and vegetables are tender. Serves 8.

Santa Fe Beef Stew

A hearty, filling soup

1½ pounds lean ground beef
1 (14 ounce) can beef broth
1 (15 ounce) can whole kernel corn with liquid
2 (15 ounce) cans pinto beans with liquid
2 (15 ounce) cans Mexican stewed tomatoes
1 tablespoon beef seasoning
1 (16 ounce) box cubed Velveeta® cheese

- In skillet, brown beef until no longer pink. Place in 5 to 6-quart slow cooker and add remaining ingredients except for cheese. Cook on LOW for 5 to 6 hours.

- When ready to serve, fold in cheese chunks and stir until cheese melts. Serves 6 to 8.

TIP: Cornbread is a must to serve with this stew.

Ol' Time Chili

2 pounds lean beef chili meat
1 large onion, finely chopped
1 (10 ounce) can chopped tomatoes and green chilies
2½ cups tomato juice
2 tablespoons chili powder
1 tablespoon ground cumin
1 tablespoon minced garlic
1 (15 ounce) can pinto or kidney beans

- In large slow cooker, combine all ingredients except pinto or kidney beans. Add 1 cup water and mix well.

- Cover and cook on LOW for 7 to 9 hours.

- Add pinto or kidney beans and continue to cook for another 30 minutes. Serves 6 to 8.

South-of-the-Border Beef Stew

1½ - 2 pounds boneless, beef chuck roast
1 green bell pepper
2 onions, coarsely chopped
2 (15 ounce) cans pinto beans with liquid
½ cup uncooked rice
1 (14 ounce) can beef broth
2 (15 ounce) cans Mexican stewed tomatoes
1 cup mild or medium green salsa
2 teaspoons ground cumin

- Trim fat from beef and cut into 1-inch cubes. In large skillet, brown beef and place in large slow cooker sprayed with vegetable cooking spray.

- Cut bell pepper into ½-inch slices and combine with remaining ingredients. Add 1½ cups water and a little salt. Cover and cook on LOW for 7 to 8 hours.

- Serve with warm flour tortillas. Serves 8.

The difference between fiction and reality?
Fiction has to make sense.

Southern Ham Stew

This is great served with cornbread.

2 cups dry black-eyed peas
3 cups cooked, cubed ham
1 large onion, chopped
2 cups sliced celery
1 (15 ounce) can yellow hominy, drained
2 (15 ounce) cans stewed tomatoes
1 (10 ounce) can chicken broth
2 teaspoons seasoned salt
2 tablespoons cornstarch

- In saucepan, rinse and drain black-eyed peas. Cover with water, bring to boil and drain again. Place in large slow cooker and add 5 cups water.

- Add ham, onion, celery, hominy, tomatoes and seasoned salt. Cover and cook on LOW for 7 to 9 hours.

- Mix cornstarch with about $\frac{1}{3}$ cup water. Turn cooker to HIGH heat and pour in cornstarch mixture and stir well.

- Cook about 10 minutes or until stew is thick and add good amount of salt and pepper. Stir well before serving. Serves 6.

TIP: If you like a little spice in the stew, substitute one can of the stewed tomatoes with one of Mexican stewed tomatoes.

When I was a boy of 14, my father was so ignorant I could hardly stand to have the old man around. But when I got to be 21, I was astonished at how much the old man had learned in seven years.
    -Mark Twain

Turkey-Veggie Chili

1 pound ground turkey
2 (15 ounce) cans pinto beans with liquid
1 (15 ounce) can great northern beans with liquid
1 (14 ounce) can chicken broth
2 (15 ounce) cans Mexican stewed tomatoes
1 (8 ounce) can whole kernel corn
1 large onion, chopped
1 red bell pepper, chopped
2 teaspoons prepared minced garlic
2 teaspoons ground cumin
½ cup uncooked elbow macaroni

- In skillet with little oil, cook turkey until brown. Place in large slow cooker.

- Add remaining ingredients except macaroni. Salt to taste and stir well. Cover and cook on LOW for 4 to 5 hours.

- Stir in macaroni and continue cooking for about 15 minutes. Stir to make sure macaroni does not stick to cooker.

- Cook additional 15 minutes or until macaroni is tender. Serves 6.

TIP: You might want to top each serving with dab of sour cream or tablespoon shredded cheddar cheese.

A friend is someone who knows the song in your heart and can sing it back to you when you have forgotten the words.
      -Anonymous

Savory Broccoli and Cauliflower

1 (16 ounce) package frozen broccoli florets, thawed
1 (16 ounce) package frozen cauliflower florets, thawed
2 (10 ounce) cans fiesta nacho cheese soup
6 slices bacon, cooked, crumbled

- Place broccoli and cauliflower in slow cooker sprayed with vegetable cooking spray.

- Sprinkle with salt and pepper and spoon soup over top. Sprinkle with bacon.

- Cover and cook on LOW for 3 to 4 hours. Serves 6.

Green Bean Revenge

2 (16 ounce) packages frozen whole green beans, thawed
2 (8 ounce) cans sliced water chestnuts, drained
1 (16 ounce) package cubed Mexican Velveeta® cheese
1 (10 ounce) can tomatoes and green chilies
¼ cup (½ stick) butter, melted
1 tablespoon chicken seasoning
1½ cups slightly crushed potato chips

- In slow cooker, combine all ingredients except crushed potato chips and mix well.

- Cover and cook on LOW for 3 to 5 hours.

- If you would like this to be a one-dish meal, add 2 to 3 cups cubed, cooked ham.

- Just before serving, cover top with crushed potato chips. Serves 8.

Beans and More Beans

4 slices thick sliced bacon, cooked crisp, crumbled
1 (15 ounce) can kidney beans, drained
1 (15 ounce) can lima beans with liquid
1 (15 ounce) can pinto beans with liquid
1 (15 ounce) can navy beans with liquid
1 (15 ounce) can pork and beans with liquid
1 onion, chopped
¾ cup chili sauce
1 cup packed brown sugar
1 tablespoon Worcestershire sauce

• In sprayed slow cooker, combine all ingredients and mix well.

• Cover and cook on LOW for 5 to 6 hours. Serves 6 to 8.

Crunchy Couscous

When rice is boring, try couscous.

1 (10 ounce) box original plain couscous
2 cups celery, sliced
1 red bell pepper, chopped
1 yellow bell pepper, chopped
1 (16 ounce) jar creamy alfredo sauce

• In 5-quart slow cooker, combine all ingredients with 1½ cups water and mix well.

• Cover and cook on LOW for 2 hours, stirring once or twice.

• Check slow cooker to ensure celery and peppers are cooked, but still crunchy. Serves 6.

Potatoes al Grande

6 medium potatoes, peeled
1 (8 ounce) package shredded cheddar cheese, divided
1 (10 ounce) can cream of chicken soup
¼ cup (½ stick) butter, melted
1 (8 ounce) carton sour cream
1 (3 ounce) can French-fried onions

- Cut potatoes into 1-inch strips and toss with salt and pepper plus 2 cups cheese. Place in slow cooker.

- Combine soup, melted butter and 2 tablespoons water and pour over potato mixture. Cover and cook on LOW for 6 to 8 hours or until potatoes are tender.

- Stir in sour cream and remaining cheese.

- When ready to serve, sprinkle fried onions over top of potatoes. Serves 8.

 The "Courthouse Steps" which is a variation of the "Log Cabin" may have been introduced as early as 1810; however, many believe it became widely popular after the Civil War. It may have been named to commemorate General Robert E. Lee's surrender to General Ulysses S. Grant in Appomattox Court House, Virginia.

Asparagus-Cheese Chicken

8 - 10 chicken thighs, skinned
2 tablespoons (¼ stick) butter
1 (10 ounce) can cream of celery soup
1 (10 ounce) can cheddar cheese soup
⅓ cup milk
1 (16 ounce) package frozen asparagus cuts

- Place chicken thighs in 5-quart slow cooker.

- In saucepan, combine butter, soups and milk and heat until butter melts. Mix well and pour over chicken thighs.

- Cover and cook on LOW for 5 to 6 hours.

- Remove cover, place asparagus cuts over chicken and cook for additional 1 hour. Serves 6 to 8.

Smothered Bacon-Wrapped Chicken

1 (3 ounce) jar dried beef
6 boneless, skinless chicken breast halves
6 slices bacon
2 (10 ounce) cans golden mushroom soup
1 (6.2 ounce) package parmesan and butter rice, cooked

- Place dried beef slices in bottom of 5-quart slow cooker.

- Roll each chicken breast half in slice of bacon and place over dried beef.

- Spoon mushroom soup and ⅓ cup water over chicken.

- Cover and cook on LOW for 7 to 8 hours. Serve over hot cooked rice. Serves 6.

Delightful Chicken and Vegetables

4 - 5 boneless skinless chicken breast halves
1 (15 ounce) can whole kernel corn, drained
1 (10 ounce) box frozen green peas, thawed
1 (16 ounce) jar alfredo sauce
1 teaspoon chicken seasoning
1 teaspoon prepared minced garlic

- In skillet, brown chicken breasts and place in oblong slow cooker sprayed with vegetable cooking spray.

- In bowl, combine remaining ingredients and spoon mixture over chicken breasts.

- Cover and cook on LOW for 4 to 5 hours.

- Serve over hot cooked pasta. Serves 4 to 5.

Tasty Chicken, Rice and Vegetables

4 boneless, skinless chicken breast halves
2 (10 ounce) jars sweet and sour sauce
1 (16 ounce) package frozen broccoli, cauliflower and carrots, thawed
1 (10 ounce) package frozen baby peas, thawed
2 cups sliced celery
1 (6 ounce) package parmesan and butter-rice mix
⅓ cup slivered almonds, toasted

- Cut chicken in 1-inch strips and combine with sweet and sour sauce and all vegetables. Place in 6-quart slow cooker sprayed with vegetable cooking spray.

- Cover and cook on LOW for 4 to 6 hours.

- When ready to serve cook parmesan-butter rice according to package directions and fold in almonds.

- Serve chicken and vegetables over hot cooked rice. Serves 4.

Chicken Delight

¾ cup white uncooked rice
1 (14 ounce) can chicken broth
1 (1 ounce) package dry onion soup mix
1 red bell pepper, seeded, chopped
2 (10 ounce) cans cream of celery soup
¾ cup white cooking wine
4 - 6 boneless, skinless chicken breasts halves
1 (3 ounce) packages fresh grated parmesan cheese

- In bowl, combine all ingredients except chicken and parmesan cheese. Add ¾ cup water and several sprinkles of black pepper and mix well. Make sure soup mixes well with liquids.

- Place chicken breast halves in 6-quart oval slow cooker sprayed well with vegetable cooking spray. Pour rice-soup mixture over chicken breasts. Cover and cook on LOW for 4 to 6 hours.

- One hour before serving, sprinkle parmesan cheese over chicken. Serves 4 to 6.

Orange Chicken

6 boneless, skinless chicken breasts halves
1 (12 ounce) jar orange marmalade
1 (8 ounce) bottle Russian dressing
1 (1 ounce) package dry onion soup mix

- Place chicken breasts in oblong slow cooker. Combine remaining ingredients and ¾ cup water. Stir well and spoon mixture over chicken breasts.

- Cover and cook on LOW for 4 to 6 hours. Serves 6.

Golden Chicken Dinner

5 boneless, skinless chicken breast halves
6 medium new potatoes with peels, cubed
6 medium carrots
1 tablespoon dried parsley flakes
1 (10 ounce) can golden mushroom soup
1 (10 ounce) can cream of chicken soup
¼ cup dried mashed potato flakes
Water or milk

- Cut chicken into ½-inch pieces.

- Place potatoes and carrots in slow cooker and top with chicken breast pieces.

- Sprinkle parsley flakes and a little salt and pepper over chicken.

- In bowl, combine soups and mix well. Spread soup mixture over chicken.

- Cover and slow cook on LOW for 6 to 7 hours.

- Stir in potato flakes and a little water or milk if necessary to make gravy. Cook another 30 minutes. Serves 5.

What happened to the very slow worker at the gum factory?

He got chewed out.

Southwestern Chicken

6 boneless, skinless chicken breast halves
1 teaspoon ground cumin
1 teaspoon chili powder
1 (10 ounce) can cream of chicken soup
1 (10 ounce) can nacho cheese soup
1 cup salsa

- In oblong slow cooker sprayed with vegetable cooking spray, place chicken sprinkled with cumin, chili powder and a little salt and pepper.

- In saucepan, combine soups and salsa and heat just enough to mix. Pour mixture over chicken breasts. Cover and cook on LOW for 6 to 7 hours.

- Serve over hot cooked rice with warmed flour tortillas spread with butter. Serves 6.

Easy Chicken Fajitas

2 pounds boneless, skinless chicken breast halves
1 onion, thinly sliced
1 red bell pepper, julienned
1 teaspoon ground cumin
1½ teaspoons chili powder
1 tablespoon lime juice
½ cup chicken broth
8 - 10 warmed flour tortillas
Guacamole and sour cream
Lettuce and tomatoes

- Cut chicken into diagonal strips and place in slow cooker sprayed with vegetable cooking spray. Top with onion and bell pepper.

- In bowl, combine cumin, chili powder, lime juice and chicken broth and pour over chicken and vegetables. Cover and cook on LOW for 5 to 7 hours.

- When serving, spoon several slices of chicken mixture with sauce into center of each warm tortilla and fold

- Serve with guacamole, sour cream, lettuce or tomatoes or plain. Serves 8.

Monterey Chicken Bake

6 (6-inch) corn tortillas
3 cups leftover chicken, cubed
1 (10 ounce) package frozen whole kernel corn
1 (15 ounce) can pinto beans with juice
1 (16 ounce) hot jar salsa
¼ cup sour cream
1 tablespoon flour
3 tablespoons snipped fresh cilantro
1 (8 ounce) package shredded 4-cheese blend

- Cut tortillas into 6 wedges. In bottom of slow cooker sprayed with vegetable cooking spray, place half wedges of tortillas.

- Place remaining wedges on cooking sheet and bake for about 10 minutes at 350°. Set aside.

- Layer chicken, corn and beans over tortillas in cooker.

- In bowl, combine salsa, sour cream, flour and cilantro and pour over corn and bean mixture. Cover and cook on LOW for 3 to 4 hours.

- When ready to serve, place baked tortillas wedges on top of each serving. Serves 8.

Missionaries introduced quilting to Hawaii in 1820. The "Echo Quilting", prominently displayed in their quilts, is said to reflect the continuous ocean waves.

Savory Chicken Fettuccine

2 pounds boneless, skinless chicken thighs, cubed
½ teaspoon garlic powder
1 red bell pepper, chopped
2 ribs celery, chopped
1 (10 ounce) can cream of celery soup
1 (10 ounce) can cream of chicken soup
1 (8 ounce) package cubed Velveeta® cheese
1 (4 ounce) jar diced pimentos
1 (16 ounce) package spinach fettuccine

- Place chicken pieces in slow cooker and sprinkle with garlic powder, a little pepper, bell pepper and celery. Top with undiluted soups.

- Cover and cook on HIGH for 4 to 6 hours or until chicken juices are clear.

- Stir in cheese and pimentos, cover and cook until cheese melts.

- Cook fettuccine according to package directions and drain. Place fettuccine in serving bowl and spoon chicken over fettuccine. Serves 8.

Hawaiian Chicken

6 skinless, boneless chicken breast halves
1 (15 ounce) can pineapple slices, reserve juice
⅓ cup packed brown sugar
2 tablespoons lemon juice
¼ teaspoon ground ginger
¼ cup cornstarch

- Place chicken breasts in sprayed oblong slow cooker and sprinkle with a little salt. Place pineapple slices over chicken.

- In bowl, mix reserved pineapple juice with remaining ingredients. Stir to mix cornstarch with liquids and pour over chicken.

- Cover and cook on LOW for 4 to 5 hours or on HIGH for 2 hours 30 minutes to 3 hours. Serve over hot buttered rice. Serves 6.

Chow Mein Chicken

4 boneless, skinless chicken breast halves
2 - 3 cups sliced celery
1 onion, coarsely chopped
$\frac{1}{3}$ cup soy sauce
$\frac{1}{4}$ teaspoon cayenne pepper
1 (14 ounce) can chicken broth
1 (16 ounce) can bean sprouts, drained
1 (8 ounce) can water chestnuts, drained
1 (6 ounce) can bamboo shoots
$\frac{1}{4}$ cup flour

- Combine chicken, celery, onion, soy sauce, cayenne pepper and chicken broth in sprayed slow cooker. Cover and cook on LOW for 3 to 4 hours.

- Add bean sprouts, water chestnuts and bamboo shoots to chicken.

- Mix flour and $\frac{1}{4}$ cup water and stir into chicken and vegetables. Cook 1 more hour. Serve over chow mein noodles. Serves 6 to 8.

Patchwork Turkey

$1\frac{1}{2}$ pounds turkey tenderloins
1 (6.2 ounce) package Oriental rice and vermicelli
1 (10 ounce) package frozen green peas, thawed
1 cup sliced celery
2 tablespoons ($\frac{1}{4}$ stick) butter, melted
1 (14 ounce) can chicken broth
$1\frac{1}{2}$ cups fresh broccoli florets

- Cut turkey tenderloins in strips. In non-stick skillet, saute turkey strips until they are no longer pink.

- In large slow cooker, combine cooked turkey strips with remaining ingredients except broccoli. Add 1 cup water and mix well.

- Cover and cook on LOW for 4 to 5 hours.

- Turn heat to HIGH setting, add broccoli and cook for another 20 minutes. Serves 8.

Beef-Noodle al Grande

1½ pounds lean ground beef
1 (16 ounce) package frozen onions and bell peppers, thawed
1 (16 ounce) box cubed Velveeta® cheese
2 (15 ounce) cans Mexican stewed tomatoes with liquid
2 (15 ounce) cans whole kernel corn, drained
1 (8 ounce) package medium egg noodles
1 cup shredded cheddar cheese

- In skillet, brown ground beef and drain fat.

- Place beef in 5 to 6-quart slow cooker, add onion, peppers, cheese, stewed tomatoes, corn and about 1 teaspoon salt and mix well. Cover and cook on LOW for 4 to 5 hours.

- Cook noodles according to package directions, drain and fold into beef-tomato mixture. Cook for another 30 minutes to heat well.

- When ready to serve, top with cheddar cheese and several sprinkles of chopped fresh parsley or chopped fresh green onions. Serves 8.

Beefy Bacon-Cheddar Supper

1 (5 ounce) box bacon and cheddar scalloped potatoes
⅓ cup milk
2 tablespoons (¼ stick) butter, melted
1 (15 ounce) can whole kernel corn with liquid
1½ pounds lean ground beef
1 onion, coarsely chopped
1 (8 ounce) package shredded cheddar cheese

- Place potatoes in sprayed slow cooker. Add 2¼ cups boiling water, milk and butter.

- Brown ground beef and onion in oil, drain and spoon over potatoes.

- Top with corn, cover and cook on LOW for 6 to 7 hours. To serve, sprinkle cheese over corn. Serves 8.

Revival Beef Stroganoff

2 pounds beef round steak
¾ cup flour, divided
½ teaspoon prepared mustard
2 onions, thinly sliced
½ pound fresh mushrooms, sliced
1 (10 ounce) can beef broth
¼ cup dry white wine or cooking win
1 (8 ounce) carton sour cream

- Trim excess fat from steak and cut into 3-inch strips about ½-inch wide.

- In bowl, combine ½ cup flour, mustard and a little salt and pepper and toss with steak strips.

- Place strips in oblong slow cooker sprayed with vegetable cooking spray and cover with onions and mushrooms. Add beef broth and wine. Cover and cook on LOW for 8 to 10 hours.

- Just before serving, combine sour cream and ¼ cup flour. Stir into cooker and cook another 10 to 15 minutes or until stroganoff is slightly thick. Serves 8.

The invention and continual revision of the sewing machine made one of the largest impacts on the sewing world. The machine was invented in the late 1700's and was used to make shoes. Elias Howe, Jr., made adjustments to accommodate lighter materials and registered it for a patent in 1846.

Tasty Pepper Steak

1½ pounds round steak
¼ cup soy sauce
1 onion, sliced
1 teaspoon prepared minced garlic
1 teaspoon sugar
¼ teaspoon ground ginger
1 (15 ounce) can stewed tomatoes
2 green bell peppers, julienned
1 teaspoon beef bouillon
1 tablespoon cornstarch

- Slice beef in strips and brown in skillet with small amount of oil. Place in oblong slow cooker.

- Add soy sauce, onion, garlic, sugar and ginger and spoon over beef. Cover and cook on LOW for 5 to 6 hours.

- Uncover, add tomatoes and green peppers and bouillon and cook 1 hour more.

- Combine cornstarch and ¼ cup water and stir into cooker. Continue cooking until liquid thickens.

- Serve over hot buttered rice or noodles. Serves 8.

In 1851, Isaac Singer improved the sewing machine and registered his patent. He later introduced the treadle designed to control the speed at which the machine stitched while allowing one to guide the fabric with both hands. His marketing plan was as inventive as his machine and by 1870 he was selling 200,000 machines a year. While a sewing machine was certainly a status symbol of the time, Singer's installment payment plan and trade-in allowance boosted sales and made his machines the most popular of the day.

Seasoned Round Steak

1 pound round steak
2 cups fresh mushrooms, halved
1 (15 ounce) can Italian stewed tomatoes
1 (10 ounce) can beef broth
½ cup red wine
2 teaspoons Italian herb seasoning
3 tablespoons quick-cooking tapioca

- Cut steak into 1-inch cubes and place in 4 to 5-quart slow cooker sprayed with cooking spray.

- Add remaining ingredients and salt and pepper, if desired.

- Cover and cook on LOW for 8 to 10 hours. Serve over hot, buttered linguine. Serves 6.

Mixed Italian Tortellini

½ pound ground round steak
1 pound bulk Italian sausage
1 (15 ounce) carton refrigerated marinara sauce
1 (15 ounce) can Italian stewed tomatoes with liquid
1½ cups sliced fresh mushrooms
1 (9 ounce) package refrigerated cheese tortellini
1½ cups shredded mozzarella cheese

- In large skillet, brown and cook ground beef about 10 minutes and drain.

- In 4 to 5-quart slow cooker, combine meat mixture, marinara sauce, tomatoes and mushrooms. Cover and cook on LOW for 6 to 8 hours.

- Stir in tortellini and sprinkle with mozzarella cheese. Turn cooker to HIGH and continue cooking for another 10 to 15 minutes or until tortellini is tender. Serves 8.

Slow-Cooker Recipes – Beef   167

Home-Style Pot Roast

1 (2 - 2½) pound boneless rump roast
5 medium potatoes, peeled, quartered
1 (16 ounce) package baby carrots, peeled
2 medium onions, quartered
1 (10 ounce) can golden mushroom soup
½ teaspoon dried basil

- In skillet lightly coated with cooking spray, brown roast on all sides.

- Place potatoes, carrots and onions in 4 to 5-quart slow cooker. Place browned roast on top of vegetables.

- In bowl, combine soup, basil and ½ teaspoon salt and pour over meat and vegetables. Cover and cook on LOW for 9 to 11 hours. Serves 8.

TIP: *When ready to serve, transfer roast and vegetables to serving dish. Stir juices remaining in slow cooker and spoon over roast and vegetables.*

Timesaver Beef Ribs and Gravy

4 - 4½ pounds beef short ribs
1 onion, sliced
1 teaspoon seasoned black pepper
1 (12 ounce) jar beef gravy
1 (1 ounce) package beef gravy mix

- Spray 6-quart slow cooker with vegetable cooking spray and place beef ribs inside. Cover with onion and sprinkle with pepper.

- In small bowl, combine beef gravy and dry gravy mix. Mix well and pour over ribs and onion. Cover and cook on LOW for 9 to 11 hours. (The ribs must cook this long on LOW to tenderize.)

- Serve with hot mashed potatoes and gravy. Serves 6.

Old-Time Pot Roast and Vegetables

1 (2 pound) chuck roast
4 - 5 medium potatoes, peeled, quartered
4 large carrots
1 onion, quartered
1 (14 ounce) can beef broth
2 tablespoons cornstarch

- Trim fat from pieces of roast and cut roast into 2 equal pieces.

- In skillet, brown pieces of roast (if desired, coat roast pieces with flour, salt and pepper).

- Spray 4 to 5-quart slow cooker with cooking spray and place potatoes, carrots and onion. Mix well.

- Place browned beef over vegetables and pour 1½ cups broth over top. Reserve and refrigerate remaining broth. Cover and cook on LOW for 8 to 9 hours.

- About 5 minutes before serving, remove beef and vegetables with slotted spoon and place on serving platter (cover to keep warm).

- Pour liquid from slow cooker into medium saucepan.

- In small bowl, blend remaining ½ cup broth and cornstarch until smooth and add to liquid in saucepan. Boil 1 minute and stir constantly.

- Serve gravy with roast and veggies and season with salt and pepper if desired. Serves 6.

We are always the same age inside.
-Gertrude Stein

Indoor Smoked Brisket

1 (4 - 6 pound) trimmed brisket
1 (4 ounce) bottle liquid smoke
Garlic salt
Celery salt
Worcestershire sauce
1 onion, chopped
1 (6 ounce) bottle barbecue sauce

- Place brisket in large shallow dish and pour liquid smoke over brisket.

- Sprinkle with garlic salt and celery salt. Cover and refrigerate overnight.

- Before cooking, drain liquid smoke and douse brisket with Worcestershire sauce.

- Place chopped onion in slow cooker and place brisket over onion. Cover and cook on LOW for 6 to 8 hours. Pour barbecue sauce over brisket and cook for additional 1 hour. Serves 8 to 10.

Sweet and Savory Brisket

1 (3 - 4 pound) trimmed beef brisket, halved
⅓ cup grape or plum jelly
1 cup ketchup
1 (1 ounce) package dry onion soup mix
¾ teaspoon black pepper

- Place half of brisket in slow cooker.

- In saucepan, combine jelly, ketchup, soup mix and black pepper and heat just enough to mix well. Spread half over brisket.

- Top with remaining brisket and jelly-soup mixture. Cover and cook on LOW for 8 to 9 hours.

- Slice brisket and serve with cooking juices. Serves 6 to 8.

Best Apricot Ham

1 (6 - 8 pound) shank ham
Whole cloves
2 tablespoons dry mustard
1¼ cups apricot jam
1¼ cups packed light brown sugar

- Place ham, fat side up, in slow cooker. Stick several whole cloves on outside of ham.

- In bowl, combine remaining ingredients and spread over ham.

- Cover and cook on LOW for 5 to 6 hours. Serves 8 to 10.

Zesty Ham Supper

1 (28 ounce) package frozen hash brown potatoes with onion and peppers, thawed
3 cups cooked, diced ham
1 (10 ounce) box frozen green peas, thawed
2 (10 ounce) cans nacho cheese soup
1 cup milk
1 bunch fresh green onions, chopped

- Place potatoes, ham and peas in 5 to 6-quart slow cooker sprayed with vegetable cooking spray. Stir lightly.

- In bowl, combine soup and milk and pour over potato mixture. Mix well.

- Cover and cook on LOW for 6 to 8 hours.

- Sprinkle green onions over top when ready to serve. Serves 8 to 10.

Tortellini Italian-Style

2 pounds bulk Italian sausage
1 (15 ounce) carton refrigerated marinara sauce
2 cups sliced fresh mushrooms, sliced
1 (15 ounce) can Italian stewed tomatoes
1 (9 ounce) package refrigerated cheese tortellini
1½ cups shredded mozzarella cheese

- In saucepan, cook Italian sausage about 10 to 15 minutes or until brown. Drain.

- In 5-quart slow cooker sprayed with vegetable cooking spray, combine sausage, marinara sauce, mushrooms and tomatoes. Cover and cook on LOW 6 to 7 hours.

- Stir in tortellini and sprinkle with cheese. Cover and cook on HIGH about 15 minutes or until tortellini is tender. Serves 8.

Italian-Herb Pork Chops

6 - 7 (1-inch) thick boneless pork chops
½ pound fresh mushrooms, sliced
1 (10 ounce) package frozen seasoned-blend onions and bell peppers, thawed
1 teaspoon Italian herb seasoning
1 (15 ounce) can Italian stewed tomatoes

- In skillet, brown pork chops on both sides and sprinkle with salt and pepper.

- In 6-quart slow cooker, combine mushrooms, seasoned-blend onions and bell peppers and seasoning.

- Place pork chops over vegetables and pour stewed tomatoes over pork chops.

- Cover and cook on LOW for 7 to 8 hours. To serve, spoon mushroom-seasoned blend over pork chops. Serves 6.

Ranch-Style Pork Chops

6 (¾-inch) bone-in pork chops
1(1 ounce) package ranch-style dressing mix
2 (15 ounce) cans new potatoes, drained, quartered
1 (10 ounce) can French onion soup

- Place pork chops in bottom of sprayed 6-quart oblong slow cooker and sprinkle with dressing mix and ½ teaspoon pepper.

- Place potatoes around pork chops and pour onion soup around potatoes and chops.

- Cover and cook on LOW for 4 to 5 hours. Serves 6.

Garden Stuffed Pork Chops

4 - 5 (1-inch) pork chops
1 (15 ounce) can mixed vegetables, well-drained
1 (8 ounce) can whole kernel corn, drained
½ cup uncooked rice
1 cup dry, Italian-style seasoned breadcrumbs
1 (15 ounce) can stewed tomatoes, slightly drained

- Cut pocket in each pork chop and season with salt and pepper.

- In large bowl, combine mixed vegetables, corn, rice and breadcrumbs. Stuff pork chops with vegetable mixture and secure open sides with toothpicks.

- Place any remaining vegetable mixture in bottom of 5-quart slow cooker. Add pork chops and spoon stewed tomatoes over top. Cover and cook on LOW for 8 to 9 hours.

- Serve vegetable mixture along with pork chops. Serves 4 to 5.

Pork Roast with Apricot Glaze

1 (3 pound) boneless pork roast
⅓ cup chicken broth
1 (18 ounce) jar apricot preserves
2 tablespoons dijon-style mustard
1 onion, finely chopped
1 green bell pepper, finely chopped

- Trim fat from roast and, if necessary, cut roast to fit into sprayed 4 to 5-quart slow cooker. Place roast in cooker.

- In saucepan, combine remaining ingredients and heat just enough to mix well. Pour over roast. Cover and cook on LOW for 9 to 11 hours or on HIGH for 5 to 6 hours. Transfer meat to serving plate.

- Sauce left in cooker is delicious as-is or thickened. To thicken, mix 1 tablespoon cornstarch and 2 tablespoons water in saucepan and add sauce from cooker. Heat, stirring constantly, until mixture thickens.

- Spoon sauce over roast or serve sauce with hot cooked rice. Serves 8.

Finger Lickin' Baby Backs

2½ - 3 pounds baby back pork ribs
½ cup chili sauce
⅓ cup apple cider vinegar
½ cup packed brown sugar

- Spray sides of 5 to 6-quart slow cooker. Cut ribs in serving-size pieces, sprinkle with pepper and place in slow cooker.

- Combine remaining ingredients and ¾ cup water. Pour over ribs.

- Cover and cook on LOW for 6 to 7 hours. After 3 hours, move ribs around in cooker to spread sauce. Serves 6 to 8.

Delectable Apricot Ribs

4 - 5 pounds baby back pork loin ribs
1 (16 ounce) jar apricot preserves
⅓ cup soy sauce
¼ cup packed light brown sugar
2 teaspoons garlic powder

- Spray large slow cooker with vegetable cooking spray and place ribs in cooker.

- In bowl, combine remaining ingredients and mix well. Spoon mixture over ribs.

- Cover and cook on LOW for 6 to 7 hours. Serves 8.

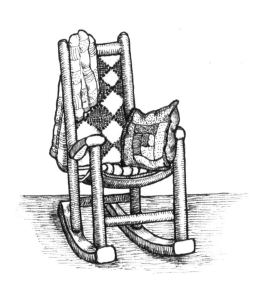

At the height of their popularity the "Log Cabin" and later the "Double Wedding Ring" patterns had so many entries at fairs that they merited their own special categories for judging.

Shrimp-Sausage Jambalaya Treasure

1 pound cooked, smoked sausage links
1 onion, chopped
1 green bell pepper, chopped
2 teaspoons minced garlic
1 (28 ounce) can diced tomatoes
1 tablespoon parsley flakes
1 teaspoon Cajun seasoning
¼ teaspoon cayenne pepper
1 pound uncooked, peeled, veined shrimp
Hot, cooked rice

- In slow cooker sprayed with vegetable cooking spray, combine all ingredients except shrimp and rice.

- Cover and cook on LOW for 6 to 8 hours or on HIGH for 3 to 4 hours.

- Stir in shrimp and cook on LOW for 1 more hour. Serve over hot, cooked rice. Serves 8.

In 1810, state and county fairs appeared throughout the country with judged categories for culinary and needlework skills. They offered a perfect venue for women to showcase their talents. The competition in the quilt division inspired quilters to combine pieced and appliqued techniques. This led to more design options while also displaying their mastery in two different quilting applications, thus improving their chance to earn a blue ribbon.

*G*roup quilts were made by family or friends and customarily given as gifts for special occasions or as a token of friendship. The sentiment of love and caring embodied in these quilts was the primary value. Antique quilts have survived as family keepsakes because they were too special for everyday use. This tradition of giving still continues today.

"Album Quilt" is given for special family occasions such as weddings, anniversaries, or birth of a child.

"Presentation Quilt" is usually given in recognition to a community figure.

"Autograph", "Signature" and "Friendship" quilts are treasured parting gifts.

Favorite block choices used in the construction of these quilts include "Chimney Sweep", "Churn Dash", and "Hole in the Barn Door." They have ample space in the center of the block for signing or embroidering one's name or a verse. The blocks are simple to piece with scrap fabric.

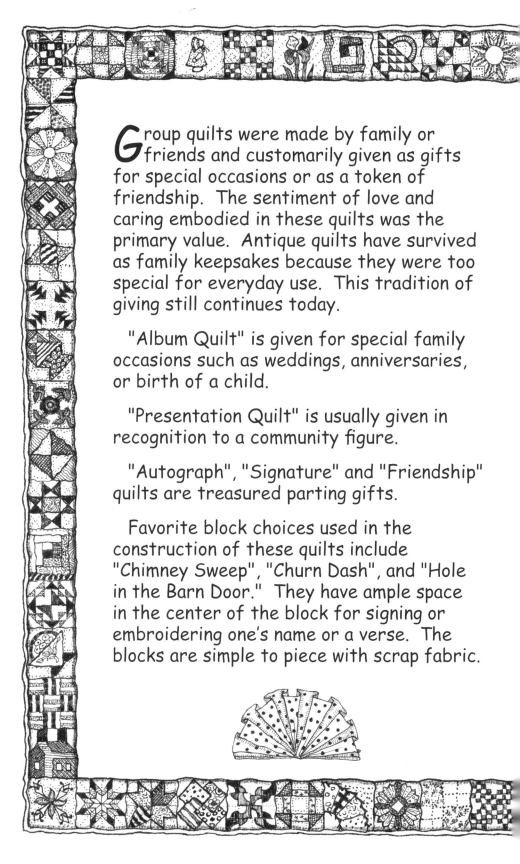

Casseroles to the Rescue

Some people come into our lives
and quickly go. Some people move
our souls to dance. They awaken
us to a new understanding with the
passing whisper of their wisdom. Some
people make the sky more beautiful to
gaze upon. They touch our lives for
awhile, leave footprints on our hearts,
and we are never, ever the same.

−Anonymous

Apple-Brunch Special

This is a really neat breakfast casserole to go along with your "bacon and eggs" and a delicious way to serve fruit with breakfast or brunch!

4 - 5 tart cooking apples, peeled, sliced
¾ cup chopped pecans
½ cup white raisins
6 tablespoons packed brown sugar
1 teaspoon ground cinnamon, divided
¼ cup (½ stick) butter
6 eggs
1½ cups orange juice
1 cup flour
3 tablespoons sugar
Extra cinnamon
Maple syrup

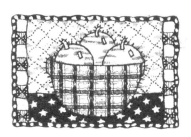

- In large skillet, saute apples, pecans, raisins, brown sugar, cinnamon and butter until apples begin to soften, about 6 minutes and stir often.

- Place in sprayed 9 x 13 inch baking dish.

- In mixing bowl, combine eggs, orange juice, flour and ¾ teaspoon salt, beat slowly until mixture is smooth and stir around edges of bowl.

- Pour over apple mixture. Sprinkle with sugar and a little cinnamon.

- Bake uncovered at 400° for about 20 to 25 minutes or until knife inserted in center of casserole comes out clean.

- Serve with maple syrup. Serves 8.

Deja moo...the feeling that you've heard this bull before.

Chiffon Cheese Souffle

Wow! This is so good. It's light and fluffy, but very rich. It must be the Old English cheese giving it that special cheese flavor. This recipe is in the Brunch section, but can easily be served for lunch. It's even good leftover and warmed up.

12 slices white bread, crusts removed
2 (5 ounce) jars Old English cheese spread, softened
6 eggs, beaten
3 cups milk
¾ cup (1½ stick) butter, melted

- (Be sure to use dish with high sides because souffle will rise and fall slightly and baking dish will be full.)

- Cut each slice of bread into 4 triangles and spoon dab of cheese on each.

- Place triangles evenly in 1 layer in sprayed 9 x 13-inch baking dish.

- In bowl, combine eggs, milk, butter and ½ teaspoon salt and mix well. Slowly pour mixture over layers of bread. Cover and refrigerate for 8 hours.

- Remove from refrigerator about 20 minutes before baking. Bake uncovered at 350° for 1 hour. Serves 8 to 10.

TIP: Be sure to use regular sliced bread and not thin slices.

The "Freedom Quilt" is one presented to a young man by his family on his 21st birthday. They were popular gifts at the turn of the 20th Century.

Overnight Breakfast

*This is "French toast" the easy way and not
just for company! The kids will love it too.*

7 cups cubed French bread, bottom crust removed
¾ cup chopped pecans
1 (3 ounce) package cream cheese, softened
¼ cup sugar
1 (8 ounce) carton whipping cream
½ cup ream maple syrup
6 eggs, slightly beaten
1 teaspoon vanilla
½ teaspoon ground cinnamon
Additional maple syrup

- Place cubed bread in sprayed 9 x 13-inch baking dish and press down gently. Sprinkle with pecans.

- In mixing bowl, beat cream cheese and sugar until fluffy and gradually mix in whipping cream and syrup.

- In separate bowl, whisk eggs, vanilla, cinnamon and ¼ teaspoon salt and fold into cream cheese-whipping cream mixture. Slowly pour this mixture evenly over bread.

- Cover and refrigerate overnight. Remove from refrigerator 20 minutes before baking.

- Bake covered at 350° for 30 minutes or until center sets and top is golden brown.

- To serve, cut into squares and serve with maple syrup. Serves 8 to 10.

Quick Breakfast Sandwiches

Wouldn't the kids love to say they had
sandwiches for breakfast! What a cool Mom!

8 slices white bread
Butter, softened
2 cups cooked, finely chopped ham
1 cup shredded Swiss cheese
3 eggs, beaten
1⅔ cup milk
1 tablespoon dried, minced onion flakes
1 teaspoon prepared mustard

- Trim crusts off bread slices. Spread butter on 1 side of each bread slice. Place 4 slices in buttered 8-inch square baking pan.

- Place chopped ham on bread slices and top with remaining bread slices, buttered side up. Sprinkle with shredded Swiss cheese.

- In bowl, combine eggs, milk, onion flakes, prepared mustard and ½ teaspoon salt and mix well. Slowly pour over bread slices and cover. Refrigerate overnight or at least 8 hours.

- Remove baking pan from refrigerator 10 minutes before cooking and bake uncovered at 325° for 30 minutes or until center sets.

- To serve, cut into 4 sandwiches. Serves 4.

TIP: Be sure to use regular sliced bread and not thin slices.

Pears cause the fewest allergic reactions of any fruit.

Sunshine on the Table

This is absolutely the prettiest casserole you'll place on your table! And it's not only pretty, but also tasty, delicious, delectable, savory, appetizing, classic and elegant. Need I go on? You'll never want a simple, buttered carrot again!

2½ cups finely shredded carrots
2 cups cooked rice
2 eggs, beaten
2 cups cubed Velveeta® cheese
1 (15 ounce) can cream-style corn
¼ cup half-and-half cream
2 tablespoons (¼ stick) butter, melted
2 tablespoons dried minced onion

- In large bowl, combine all ingredients and a little salt and pepper and mix well.

- Spoon mixture into sprayed 3-quart baking dish.

- Bake uncovered at 350° for 40 minutes or until set. Serves 8.

Collecting autographs was a popular pastime for young men and women in the mid-1800's. It is believed that this craze influenced the introduction of "Album Quilts."

Green Bean Delight

¼ cup (½ stick) butter, divided
½ cup onion, chopped
½ cup celery, chopped
1 tablespoon flour
1 teaspoon sugar
1 cup half-and-half cream
3 (15 ounce) cans French-style green beans, drained
¾ cup crushed corn flakes
1 cup shredded Swiss cheese

• Melt 2 tablespoons butter in skillet and saute onion and celery. Stir in flour, sugar, and ½ teaspoon each of salt and pepper. Cook 1 minute on medium heat. Stir constantly.

• Reduce heat and slowly add cream and stir until smooth. Cook and stir over low heat about 2 minutes until mixture is thick, but do not boil. Fold in green beans.

• Spread mixture into sprayed 9 x 13-inch baking dish.

• Melt remaining butter and toss with cornflake crumbs. Mix in cheese and sprinkle mixture over top of casserole.

• Bake uncovered at 325° for 25 minutes or until it heats thoroughly. Serves 8 to 10.

A "sampler" quilt is a collection of different patterns usually connected with sashing.

Spicy Vegetable Couscous

This is a really good dish and also very colorful and attractive.

1 (5.7 ounce) package herbed-chicken couscous
3 tablespoons butter
3 tablespoons oil
1 small yellow squash, diced
1 small zucchini, diced
½ red onion, diced
1 red bell pepper, diced
1 (10 ounce) box frozen green peas, thawed
½ teaspoon garlic powder
½ teaspoon ground cumin
½ teaspoon curry powder
¼ teaspoon cayenne pepper
1½ cups shredded mozzarella cheese

- Cook couscous according to package directions, but add 3 tablespoons butter instead of amount specified.

- In large skillet, heat oil and saute squash, zucchini, onion and bell pepper about 10 minutes but do not brown. Add peas, garlic powder, cumin, curry powder, cayenne pepper and ½ teaspoon salt to mixture and toss well.

- Combine vegetables and couscous. If it seems a little dry, add few tablespoons water.

- Pour into sprayed 2½-quart baking dish and sprinkle with mozzarella cheese.

- Bake covered at 350° for about 25 minutes. Serves 8.

TIP: This may be refrigerated and heated later. Set at room temperature for about 30 minutes before heating. If you prefer a milder hot, use only ⅛ teaspoon red pepper.

Yummy Asparagus-Cheese Bake

3 (15 ounce) cans cut asparagus spears with liquid
3 eggs, hard-boiled, chopped
½ cup chopped pecans
1 (10 ounce) can condensed cream of asparagus soup
¼ cup (½ stick) butter
2 cups cracker crumbs
1 (8 ounce) package shredded Monterey Jack cheese

- Drain asparagus spears and set aside liquid. Arrange asparagus spears in sprayed 2-quart casserole dish and top with chopped eggs and pecans.

- In saucepan, heat asparagus soup with asparagus liquid, butter and a little pepper. Pour over asparagus spears, eggs and pecans.

- Combine cracker crumbs and cheese and sprinkle over casserole. Bake uncovered at 350° for 25 minutes. Serves 8.

Home-Style Broccoli Casserole

1 small onion, chopped
2 (10 ounce) packages frozen chopped broccoli, thawed, drained
1 (10 ounce) can cream of mushroom soup
1 (8 ounce) carton sour cream
1 (6 ounce) package stuffing mix
½ cup (1 stick) butter, melted

- Preheat oven to 350°. In small skillet with a little oil, saute onion.

- In large bowl, combine sauted onion, broccoli, soup and sour cream. Mix well.

- In separate bowl, combine stuffing mix and melted butter and mix well. Place ½ stuffing mixture in sprayed 9 x 13-inch baking dish. Top with broccoli-soup mixture and spread with back of spoon.

- Spoon remaining stuffing mixture, cover and bake for 30 minutes. Remove cover and cook for additional 10 minutes. Serves 8.

Blue Ribbon Potato Casserole

This is a "winner" for the best potato casserole you'll ever make! It is a particular favorite of the men!

1 (2 pound) bag frozen hash brown potatoes, thawed
1 onion, finely chopped
¾ cup (1½ stick) butter, melted, divided
1 (8 ounce) carton sour cream
1 (10 ounce) can cream of chicken soup
1 (8 ounce) package shredded cheddar cheese
2 cups crushed corn flakes

- In large mixing bowl, combine hash browns, onion, ½ cup (1 stick) melted butter, sour cream, soup and cheese and mix well. Pour into sprayed 9 x 13-inch baking dish.

- In separate bowl, combine corn flakes and ¼ cup (½ stick) melted butter.

- Sprinkle mixture over top of casserole and bake uncovered at 350° for 45 to 50 minutes or until bubbly around edges. Serves 10.

10 Good Reasons to Have Meals at Home are included in this cookbook. Here's one of them.

8. Family meals reduce the risk of obesity and substance abuse. Family meals are more nutritious than fast food drive-through places. You can choose the food, control portions of food as well as use less fat, less salt, less sugar and fewer calories.

Sweet Potato Casserole

*This is a beautiful Thanksgiving dish and perfect
for Christmas dinner, too. Even people who are
"lukewarm" about sweet potatoes will like this casserole.*

1 (29 ounce) can sweet potatoes, drained
⅓ cup evaporated milk
¾ cup sugar
¼ cup packed brown sugar
2 eggs, beaten
¼ cup (½ stick) butter, melted
1 teaspoon vanilla

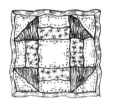

Topping:

1 cup packed light brown sugar
¼ cup (½ stick) butter, melted
½ cup flour
1 cup chopped pecans

- Place sweet potatoes in mixing bowl and mash slightly with fork.

- Add evaporated milk, sugar, eggs, butter and vanilla and mix well.

- Pour into sprayed 7 x 11-inch baking dish or 2-quart baking dish.

- For topping, combine brown sugar, butter and flour in bowl and mix well.

- Stir in chopped pecans and sprinkle over casserole.

- Bake uncovered at 350° for 35 minutes or until crusty on top. Serves 8 to 10.

*A "Sampler Friendship Quilt" allows each
signer to select the block they want to make
and autograph.*

Garden Spinach-Artichoke Casserole

2 (10 ounce) packages frozen chopped spinach, thawed, well-drained
1 (14 ounce) can artichoke hearts, drained, chopped
1 (16 ounce) carton half-and-half cream, divided
¾ cup grated parmesan cheese
1 (8 ounce) package cream cheese, softened

- Preheat oven to 350°. Drain spinach well (squeeze dry with paper towels). In bowl, combine spinach, artichoke, ⅔ cup cream, half parmesan and generous sprinkling of salt and pepper. Pour into sprayed 7 x 11-inch baking dish.

- In mixing bowl, beat cream cheese until fluffy and scrape sides of bowl with rubber spatula. Reduce speed and gradually mix in remaining cream. Pour over spinach mixture and sprinkle with remaining parmesan cheese.

- Bake uncovered for 35 minutes or until edges bubble and top is light brown. Serves 8.

10 Good Reasons to Have Meals at Home are included in this cookbook. Here's one of them.

9. Family meals help children learn about different foods, how to make food choices and about your ideas about food so they can live healthy lives. When children see you make good food choices, they will mimic your actions.

Favorite Spinach Enchiladas

*Wow, these are good! These enchiladas are
great and so much fun to make and serve.*

2 (10 ounce) boxes chopped spinach, thawed, pressed dry
1 (1 ounce) package dry onion soup mix
3 cups shredded cheddar cheese, divided
3 cups shredded Monterey Jack cheese or mozzarella, divided
12 flour tortillas
1 pint whipping cream or half-and-half cream

- Drain spinach well on several paper towels.

- In medium bowl, combine spinach and soup mix. Blend in
  1½ cup cheddar cheese and 1½ cup Monterey Jack cheese.

- Spread out 12 tortillas and place about 3 heaping tablespoons
  spinach mixture down middle of each tortilla and roll up.

- Place each filled tortilla, seam side down, in sprayed
  10 x 14-inch baking dish.

- Pour whipping cream over enchiladas and sprinkle with
  remaining cheeses. Cover and bake at 350° for 20 minutes.
  Uncover and bake another 10 minutes longer. Serves 8 to 10.

*TIP: This recipe will freeze well. To make ahead of time, freeze
before adding whipping cream and remaining cheeses. Thaw in
refrigerator before cooking. Eat them all up because tortillas
get a little tough when reheated.*

*Early quilters traded patterns with one another
and made cloth sample blocks. These blocks
were kept together and used as a reference for
future quilting projects.*

Festive Cranberries

What a great dish for Thanksgiving or Christmas!

2 (20 ounce) cans pie apples
1 (16 ounce) can whole cranberries
¾ cup sugar
½ cup packed brown sugar

Topping:

¼ cup (½ stick) butter
1½ cups crushed corn flakes
⅔ cup sugar
½ teaspoon ground cinnamon
1 cup chopped pecans

- In bowl, combine pie apples, cranberries and both sugars and mix well. Spoon into sprayed 2-quart baking dish.

- In saucepan, melt butter and mix in oats, flour, sugar, cinnamon and pecans. Sprinkle mixture over apples and cranberries and bake uncovered at 325° for 1 hour.

- This can be served hot or at room temperature. Serves 8.

TIP: Look for pie apples, not apple pie filling.

An excellent health tip: Dream More While You Are Awake.

Maple-Bean Supper

2 (15 ounce) cans pork and beans with juice
1 (15 ounce) can navy beans, drained
1 (15 ounce) can butter beans, drained
1 (15 ounce) can pinto beans with jalapenos, drained
3 cups chopped, leftover ham

Sauce:

$\frac{2}{3}$ cup maple syrup (not light syrup)
$\frac{1}{3}$ cup ketchup
2 tablespoons white vinegar
2 tablespoons prepared mustard

- Preheat oven to 350°. In large bowl, combine all beans and stir in ham.

- In saucepan, combine all sauce ingredients and heat well.

- Pour over bean-ham mixture and mix well. Transfer to sprayed 2$\frac{1}{2}$-quart glass baking dish. Cover and bake for 35 minutes or until bubbly around edges. Serves 8 to 10.

Godey's Lady's Book *was a leader in publishing quilt patterns as early as 1835. The first pattern published was the hexagon, which was a popular English pattern. Magazines and newspapers followed suit and later began to name the patterns.*

Confetti Orzo

*This is really good. The alfredo sauce gives it a mild,
pleasing flavor. (It sure beats regular "buttered rice".)*

8 ounces orzo pasta
½ cup (1 stick) butter
3 cups stemmed broccoli florets
1 bunch green onions with tops, chopped
1 red bell pepper, seeded, chopped
2 cups chopped celery
1 clove garlic, minced
½ teaspoon cumin
2 teaspoons chicken bouillon
1 (8 ounce) carton sour cream
1 (16 ounce) jar creamy alfredo sauce

- Cook orzo according to package directions;
  however, it is best to stir orzo several times
  during cooking time. Drain.

- While orzo is cooking, melt butter in skillet
  and saute broccoli, onions, bell pepper, celery, garlic and
  cumin and cook just until tender-crisp. Add chicken bouillon
  to vegetables.

- Spoon vegetable mixture into large bowl and add sour cream,
  alfredo sauce, orzo, and a little salt and pepper. Spoon this
  mixture into sprayed 9 x 13-inch baking dish.

- This is ready to cook, but you may refrigerate it and
  cook later.

- After it has come to room temperature, cook covered at
  325° for 30 minutes. Serves 8.

*TIP: This can easily be made into a main dish by adding 3 to 4 cups
      chopped, cooked chicken or turkey.*

Spinach-Cheese Manicotti

*This does take extra time to fill shells, but it is
really a special dish and worth the time it takes!*

1 onion, minced
2 teaspoons minced garlic
2 tablespoons oil
1 (15 ounce) carton ricotta cheese
1 (3 ounce) package cream cheese, softened
1 (8 ounce) package shredded mozzarella cheese, divided
1 (3 ounce) package grated parmesan cheese, divided
2 teaspoons Italian herb seasoning
1 (10 ounce) box frozen chopped spinach, thawed, drained
9 manicotti shells, cooked, drained on wax paper
1 (26 ounce) jar spaghetti sauce

- In skillet, saute onion and garlic in oil and set aside.

- In mixing bowl, combine ricotta, cream cheese, half
  mozzarella, half parmesan, Italian seasoning, and ½ teaspoon
  each of salt and pepper and beat until they blend well.

- Drain spinach on several paper towels and squeeze until
  spinach drains well.

- Add spinach and onion to cheese mixture and mix well. Spoon
  this mixture into manicotti shells using 1 teaspoon at a time.
  (Be careful not to tear shells.)

- Pour half spaghetti sauce in bottom of sprayed 9 x 13-inch
  baking dish. Arrange shells over sauce and top with remaining
  sauce. Cover and bake at 350° for 30 minutes.

- Remove from oven, uncover and sprinkle remaining cheeses
  over top. Return to oven just until cheese melts. Serves 9.

Delightful Chicken Souffle

This is a fabulous dish for a luncheon. It is really easy to make and you may make it the day before. Serve with an English pea salad and slice of cantaloupe or honeydew melon. You don't even need bread with this casserole.

16 slices white bread, crusts removed
5 boneless, skinless, chicken breast halves, cooked, thinly
   sliced diagonally
½ cup mayonnaise
1 cup grated cheddar cheese, divided
5 large eggs
2 cups milk
1 (10 ounce) can cream of mushroom soup

- Spray 9 x 13-inch baking dish. Line bottom with 8 slices of bread, buttered on 1 side. Cover with sliced chicken. (You can use deli-sliced chicken instead of cooking chicken breasts.)

- Spread mayonnaise over chicken slices and sprinkle with ½ cup cheese. Top with remaining 8 slices bread.

- In mixing bowl, beat eggs, milk, and ½ teaspoon each of salt and pepper and pour over entire casserole. Refrigerate all day or overnight.

- When ready to bake, spread mushroom soup over top casserole using back of large spoon.

- Bake covered at 350° for 45 minutes.

- Uncover, sprinkle with remaining ½ cup cheddar cheese, return to oven and bake for another 15 minutes. Serves 10.

He, who can protest and does not, is an accomplice in the act.
                                        -The Talmud

Spectacular Chicken Spaghetti

This recipe is a different twist on the popular chicken spaghetti. To give it more of a twist, use chopped, cooked ham instead of chicken. What a wonderful casserole to serve family or company. It has great flavor and taste with chicken, pasta and colorful vegetables all in one.

It's a winner, I promise!

1 bunch fresh green onions and tops, chopped
1 cup chopped celery
1 red bell pepper, chopped
1 yellow or orange bell pepper, chopped
¼ cup (½ stick) butter
1 tablespoon dried cilantro leaves
1 teaspoon Italian herb seasoning
1 (7 ounce) package thin spaghetti,
   cooked, drained
4 cups chopped, cooked chicken or turkey
1 (8 ounce) carton sour cream
1 (16 ounce) jar creamy alfredo sauce
1 (10 ounce) box frozen green peas, thawed
1 (8 ounce) package shredded mozzarella
   cheese, divided

- In large skillet, saute onions, celery and bell peppers in butter.

- In large bowl, combine onion-pepper mixture, seasonings, spaghetti, chicken, sour cream, alfredo sauce, 2 teaspoons salt and 1 teaspoon pepper and mix well.

- Fold in peas and half mozzarella cheese.

- Spoon into sprayed 10 x 14-inch deep casserole dish and bake covered at 350° for 45 minutes.

- Remove from oven and sprinkle remaining cheese over casserole. Return to oven for about 5 minutes. Serves 10.

TIP: With spaghetti dishes like this, I like to break up spaghetti before cooking it. It just makes it a bit easier to serve and eat.

Great Crazy Chicken Lasagna

Chicken never got mixed up with any better ingredients!

1 tablespoon butter
½ onion, chopped
1 cup fresh mushrooms, sliced
1 (10 ounce) can condensed cream of chicken soup
1 (16 ounce) jar alfredo sauce
1 (4 ounce) jar diced pimentos, drained
⅓ cup dry, white wine
1 (10 ounce) package frozen chopped spinach, well-drained
1 (15 ounce) carton ricotta cheese
⅓ cup grated parmesan cheese
1 egg, beaten
9 lasagna cooked noodles
3 - 4 cups cooked, shredded chicken
1 (16 ounce) package shredded cheddar cheese

- In large skillet, melt butter and saute onion and mushrooms. Stir in soup, alfredo sauce, pimentos and wine. Set aside one-third sauce for top of lasagna.

- Drain spinach with layers of paper towels. (Spinach needs to be completely drained.)

- In bowl, combine spinach, ricotta, parmesan and egg and mix well.

- Place 3 noodles in sprayed 10 x 15-inch baking dish. Make sure baking dish is full-size with depth of 2½ inches.

- Layer each with half of remaining sauce, spinach-ricotta mixture and chicken. (Spinach-ricotta mixture will be fairly dry so you will have to spoon it over sauce and spread it out.)

- Sprinkle with 1½ cups cheddar cheese. Repeat layering.

- Top with last 3 noodles and reserved sauce. Cover and bake at 350° for 45 minutes.

- Remove from oven and sprinkle remaining cheese on top.

- Return to oven uncovered and bake another 5 minutes or just until cheese melts. Let casserole stand 10 minutes before serving. Serves 12.

Hurry-Up Chicken Enchiladas

This is a fast and fun way to make a dish with ingredients at your fingertips. It's also a great dish for kids to make.

2½ - 3 cups shredded cooked chicken breasts
1 (10 ounce) can cream of chicken soup with juice
2 cups chunky salsa, divided
8 (6-inch) flour tortillas
1 (10 ounce) can nacho cheese soup

* In saucepan, combine chicken (or substitute turkey), soup and ½ cup salsa. Heat on LOW and stir constantly so mixture will not burn.

* Spread flour tortillas on counter and spoon about ⅓ cup chicken mixture down center of each tortilla.

* Roll tortilla around filling and place, seam-side down, in sprayed 9 x 13-inch baking dish.

* In saucepan, combine cheese soup, remaining salsa and ¼ cup water. Heat just enough so mixture can be poured and pour over enchiladas.

* Cover with wax paper and microwave on HIGH for 4 to 5 minutes or until bubbly. Turn several times. Serves 6 to 8.

The "House" block has several variations and has been in existence since the 1840's. The popular "Schoolhouse Block" is thought to have originated in New Jersey during the early 1870's.

Cabbage-Beef Rolls

This is a wonderful family recipe and a great way for kids to eat cabbage. Anyone who has ever had a garden has probably made some version of these well-loved cabbage rolls.

1 large head cabbage, cored
1½ pounds lean ground beef
1 egg, beaten
3 tablespoons ketchup
⅓ cup dry, seasoned breadcrumbs
2 tablespoons dried, minced onion flakes
2 (15 ounce) cans Italian stewed tomatoes
¼ cup cornstarch
3 tablespoons packed brown sugar
2 tablespoons Worcestershire sauce

- In large pot, place cabbage in boiling water 10 minutes or until outer leaves are tender. Drain well. Rinse in cold water and remove 10 large outer leaves. (To get that many large leaves, you may have to arrange 2 smaller leaves together to make one roll). Set aside.

- Take remaining cabbage and slice or grate in slivers. Place in sprayed 9 x 13-inch baking dish.

- In large bowl, combine ground beef, egg, ketchup, breadcrumbs, onion flakes and 1 teaspoon salt and mix well.

- Place about ½ cup meat mixture packed together on each cabbage leaf.

- Fold in sides and roll up leaf to completely enclose filling. (You may have to remove thick vein from cabbage leaves for easier rolling.) Place each rolled leaf over grated cabbage.

- In large saucepan, pour stewed tomatoes. Combine cornstarch, brown sugar and Worcestershire sauce and spoon mixture into tomatoes. Cook on high heat, stir constantly until mixture is thick. Pour mixture over cabbage rolls.

- Cover and bake at 325° for 1 hour. Serves 8.

Super Spaghetti Pie

This is a great recipe to make ahead of time! Have it ready for a late supper after a game or a midnight supper when teenagers demand "food"! What better than "food" that resembles pizza?

6 ounces spaghetti
⅓ cup grated parmesan cheese
1 egg, beaten
1 tablespoon butter, melted
1 cup small-curd cottage cheese, drained
½ pound lean ground beef
½ pound sausage
½ cup chopped onion
1 (15 ounce) can tomato sauce
1 teaspoon garlic powder
1 tablespoon sugar
1 teaspoon oregano
½ cup shredded mozzarella cheese

- In large pan, cook spaghetti according to package directions. Drain well.

- While spaghetti is still warm, stir in cheese, egg and butter in large bowl.

- Pour into sprayed 10-inch pie plate and pat mixture up and around sides with spoon to form crust. Spoon cottage cheese over spaghetti crust.

- In skillet, brown ground beef, sausage and chopped onion. Drain off fat and add tomato sauce, garlic powder, sugar, oregano, and ½ teaspoon each of salt and pepper. Simmer for 10 minutes and stir occasionally.

- Spoon meat mixture over cottage cheese and bake at 350° for 30 minutes.

- Arrange mozzarella on top and return to oven just until cheese melts. Serves 8.

Ham and Cheesy Rice Casserole

1 (5 ounce) package parmesan rice and vermicelli mix
2 cups cubed cooked ham
1 (15 ounce) can whole kernel corn, drained
1 (15 ounce) can cut green beans, drained
1 (6 ounce) can cheesy French-fried onions, divided

- Preheat oven to 350°. Cook rice and vermicelli mix according to package directions.

- In large bowl, combine cooked rice and vermicelli, ham, corn, green beans and half fried onions.

- Spoon into sprayed 9 x 13-inch baking pan, cover and bake for 25 minutes. Uncover and sprinkle remaining onions over top of casserole.

- Return to oven for 10 to 15 minutes or until onions are light brown. Serves 8.

Walnut-Ham Linguine

2 teaspoons minced garlic
½ cup coarsely chopped walnuts
1 red bell pepper, julienned
¼ cup olive oil
½ pound cooked ham, cut in strips
1 (16 ounce) jar creamy alfredo sauce
¼ cup grated parmesan cheese
1 (12 ounce) package linguine, cooked al dente
1 cup dry, seasoned breadcrumbs

- In large skillet, saute garlic, walnuts and bell pepper in oil for 1 to 2 minutes.

- In large bowl, combine garlic mixture with ham, alfredo sauce, cheese and linguine. Mix well and spoon into sprayed 3-quart casserole dish.

- Sprinkle breadcrumbs over top and bake uncovered at 350° for   35 minutes or until breadcrumbs are light brown. Serves 8.

Fiesta Pork Casserole

This zesty casserole is so easy to put together and it really gets your attention! It is an especially nice change of pace from the usual Mexican dish using ground beef.

2 pounds boneless pork tenderloin
1 onion, chopped
1 green bell pepper, chopped
3 tablespoons oil
1 (15 ounce) can black beans, rinsed, drained
1 (10 ounce) can nacho cheese soup
1 (15 ounce) can stewed tomatoes
1 (4 ounce) can diced green chilies
1 cup instant brown rice, cooked
¾ cup salsa
2 teaspoons ground cumin
¾ cup shredded Mexican 3-cheese blend

- Cut pork in 1-inch cubes. In very large skillet, brown pork, onion and bell pepper in oil until pork is no longer pink. Drain well.

- Add beans, cheese soup, stewed tomatoes, green chilies, rice, salsa, cumin and ½ teaspoon salt. Cook on medium heat and stir occasionally until mixture is bubbly.

- Spoon into buttered 4-quart baking dish and bake uncovered at 350° for 30 minutes or until bubbly around edges.

- Remove from oven and sprinkle with cheese. Let stand few minutes before serving. Serves 8 to 10.

He who blesses most is blest.
-John Greenleaf Whittier

Pork-Vegetable Noodle Bake

1½ - 2 pounds pork tenderloin
3 tablespoons oil
2 cups celery, chopped
1 red bell pepper, seeded, chopped
1 green bell pepper, seeded, chopped
1 onion, chopped
1 (4 ounce) can sliced mushrooms
1 (10 ounce) can tomatoes and green chilies
1 (10 ounce) can cream of mushroom soup with garlic
1 (10 ounce) can cream of celery soup
¼ cup soy sauce
1 (7 ounce) package elbow macaroni, cooked, drained
2 cups chow mein noodles

- Cut pork into 1-inch cubes. In skillet, brown pork in oil and cook on low heat for about 15 minutes. With slotted spoon, remove pork to side dish.

- Saute celery, bell peppers and onion in same skillet in remaining oil.

- In large bowl, combine pork, celery-onion mixture, mushrooms, tomatoes and green chilies, soups, soy sauce and macaroni.

- Spoon casserole into sprayed 9 x 13-inch baking dish or 2 smaller baking dishes.

- Top with chow mein noodles and bake uncovered at 350° for 50 minutes. Serves 8 to 10.

TIP: If you make 2 smaller casseroles, you may freeze one. Wait to sprinkle chow mein noodles over casserole until just before placing in the oven to cook.

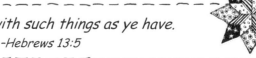

Be content with such things as ye have.
-Hebrews 13:5

Pork Chop-Cheddar Bake

8 boneless pork chops
1 (10 ounce) can cream of mushroom soup
1 cup uncooked rice
1½ cups shredded cheddar cheese, divided
½ cup minced onion
⅓ cup chopped bell pepper
1 (4 ounce) can sliced mushrooms, drained
1 (3 ounce) can French-fried onions

- In large skillet, cook and brown pork chops. Drain well and place in sprayed 9 x 13-inch baking dish.

- In same skillet, combine soup, 1½ cups water, rice, ½ cup cheese, onion, bell pepper and mushrooms and mix well. Pour mixture over pork chops.

- Cover with foil and bake at 325° for 1 hour 10 minutes.

- Uncover and top with remaining cheese and fried onions.

- Return to oven just until cheese melts. Serves 8.

 During the mid-1800's, the "Dresden Plate" was named to commemorate the first china factory in Europe.
*   The block has 16 to 20 spokes that can either be rounded or pointed. The pointed version is called the "Sunflower Block." This pattern is also known as the "Friendship Block" because the center circle has ample space for signing one's name for use in a "Friendship Quilt."*

No Noodle Tuna

1(8 ounce) tube refrigerated crescent rolls
1 cup shredded white cheddar cheese
1 (10 ounce) box frozen chopped broccoli, thawed
4 eggs, beaten
1 (2 ounce) box cream of broccoli soup mix
1 (8 ounce) carton sour cream
1 cup milk
½ cup mayonnaise
2 tablespoons dried onion flakes
½ teaspoon dill weed
2 (6 ounce) cans white meat tuna, drained, flaked
1 (2 ounce) jar diced pimentos

- Unroll crescent dough into 1 long rectangle and place in unsprayed 9 x 13-inch baking dish. Seal seams and press into bottom and ½ inch up sides.

- Sprinkle with cheese and chopped broccoli.

- In bowl, combine eggs, broccoli soup mix, sour cream, milk, mayonnaise, onion flakes and dill weed and mix well. Stir in tuna and pimentos.

- Pour over broccoli-cheese in baking dish and bake covered at 350° for 40 minutes or until knife inserted near center comes out clean.

- Cut into squares to serve. Serves 8.

If your sister hits you, don't hit her back. They always catch the second person.

Crunchy Orange Roughy

½ cup (1 stick) butter, divided
1 red bell pepper, chopped
1 onion, chopped
¼ cup flour
1 teaspoon basil
1 (16 ounce) carton half-and-half cream
1 (3 ounce) package grated parmesan cheese
1 tablespoon marinade for chicken
1½ pounds orange roughy fillets
3 hard-boiled eggs, sliced
1½ cups round buttery cracker crumbs

- In skillet, melt ¼ cup butter and saute bell pepper and onion. Add flour, basil, and ½ teaspoon each of salt and pepper. Cook on medium heat about 2 minutes. Slowly add half-and-half cream and stir constantly until mixture becomes thick. Stir in parmesan cheese and marinade for chicken.

- In another skillet, melt 2 tablespoons butter and brown orange roughy fillet. Transfer to sprayed 9 x 13-inch baking dish and place egg slices over fish.

- Pour cream sauce over eggs and fillets and bake uncovered at 350° for 15 minutes.

- Combine cracker crumbs and remaining 2 tablespoons butter. Sprinkle crumbs over casserole and bake another 10 to 15 minutes or until crumbs are light brown. Serves 8.

TIP: You may substitute any white fish for the orange roughy.

To err is human; to forgive is divine.
-Alexander Pope

The "Crazy Quilt" was the rage of the late 1800's. It was made by stitching irregular scraps of luxurious silks, brocades, taffetas, and velvets onto a fabric foundation square. Many companies, especially tobacco, gave premium or promotional gifts of silk ribbons or squares with famous figures painted on them. These also found their way into the opulent quilts.

Quilters did not stop here but further embellished their masterpiece with elaborate embroidery stitches. Most of these designs were traced from magazines or whatever caught their fancy. These quilts may have embroidered versions of the first "Sunbonnet Sue" tucked in among birds, butterflies, baskets, flowers and, of course, a spider in its web for good luck.

Magazines offered complete kits containing pre-stamped fabric and silk embroidery thread. These Victorian quilts were often finished with the crowning touch of a ruffled border.

Show-Stopper Sweets

*May love and laughter light
your days and warm your heart
and home. May good and faithful
friends be yours where ever you may
roam. May peace and plenty bless your
world with joy that long endures. May
all life's passing seasons bring the best
to you and yours.*

                                    –Irish Blessing

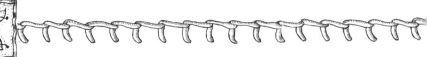

Spectacular Gift Jars Made Easy

Use your imagination to create fun, easy and personalized gifts! This is an excellent craft project for anyone and even your little ones can help paint, glue and decorate. Gather your supplies and enjoy time together. Here are a few quick ideas and pointers.

Top It!

(Jar topper should always be secured with a rubber band.)

- Spray paint the lid and decorate with buttons, charms, beads or old costume jewelry.

- Cut 2 (6½ to 7-inch) squares of coordinating fabric. Place first square on top of the second so that the points are centered on the straight edge. The catty-corner placement produces a cute handkerchief hem and gives your friend fabric squares for her stash.

- Use those extra blocks from former projects as lid toppers. This is a great idea for a cookie-block exchange to make gifts extra special.

- Place jar inside a simple, fabric drawstring bag. Use novelty prints for holidays or special events.

Tie It!

(Ribbon, Wired Ribbon, Jute, Cording, Raffia or Fabric)

- Narrow ribbon – conceal rubber band by wrapping the jar lid with several strands of narrow ribbon in the same or complimentary colors and tie in a bow. Knot each ribbon streamer a few times at different intervals for added interest.

- For a cute idea with narrow ribbon, select an antique or unique button, pull ribbon ends through the button holes and tie in a bow or knot.

- Wired ribbon or garland (stars, snowflakes, hearts, etc.) – conceal rubber band by wrapping the jar lid several times with ribbon or garland and twist to secure. Leave 6-inch streamers on both sides of the wire garland. Coil each end around a pencil to form a curl.

- Cording – loop small tassels around the cording for an extra touch. Be sure to knot ends of cording streamers for a great look.

- Fabric – cut fabric in 2-inch strips, fold lengthwise and wrap over rubber band. Tie in a bow or knot. Glue buttons, charms, beads or other embellishments as desired.

Tag It!

(Each recipe has 3 tags, which include the baking instructions.)

- Photocopy or simply cut tags from the book and attach to the jar.

- Use colored pens to add a little zip to the art already on the tag.

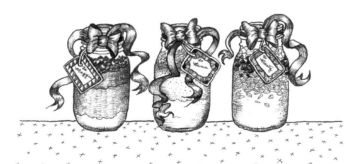

Deluxe Oatmeal Cookies

Oatmeal cookies chock full of sweet cranberries, crunchy walnuts and tasty dates will entice everyone's taste buds.

Ingredients for jar:

⅓ cup sugar
⅓ cup packed light brown sugar
½ cup flour
½ teaspoon baking soda
1 cup quick-cooking oats
½ cup dried, sweetened cranberries
1 cup coarsely chopped walnuts
½ cup chopped dates

Instructions for filling jar:

- Pour sugar into 1-quart jar and smooth over.
- Spoon brown sugar over sugar and pack down firmly but evenly.
- Spoon flour and baking soda over brown sugar and press down.
- Pour in oats and then place cranberries on oats.
- Place walnuts over cranberries and press down.
- Add dates over walnuts and place lid on jar to close.

Instructions for baking:

⅓ cup (5⅓ tablespoons) butter, softened
1 egg
½ teaspoon vanilla

- Preheat oven to 350°. Empty contents of jar into large mixing bowl. Add butter, egg and vanilla.

- Beat on LOW speed until dough blends thoroughly.

- Roll heaping teaspoonfuls of dough into balls and place 3 inches apart on cookie baking sheet.

- Bake for 12 to 14 minutes or until edges are light brown. Remove from oven and let cookies cool for 1 minute before transferring to cooling rack. (Yields 3 to 3½ dozen.)

Deluxe Oatmeal Cookies

⅓ cup (5⅓ tablespoons) butter, softened
1 egg
½ teaspoon vanilla

- Preheat oven to 350°. Empty contents of jar into large mixing bowl. Add butter, egg and vanilla.
- Beat on LOW speed until dough blends thoroughly.
- Roll heaping teaspoonful of dough into balls and place 3 inches apart on cookie baking sheet.
- Bake for 12 to 14 minutes or until edges are light brown. Remove from oven and let cookies cool for 1 minute before transferring to cooling rack. (Yields 3 to 3½ dozen.)

www.cookbookresources.com

— —

Deluxe Oatmeal Cookies

⅓ cup (5⅓ tablespoons) butter, softened
1 egg
½ teaspoon vanilla

- Preheat oven to 350°. Empty contents of jar into large mixing bowl. Add butter, egg and vanilla.
- Beat on LOW speed until dough blends thoroughly.
- Roll heaping teaspoonful of dough into balls and place 3 inches apart on cookie baking sheet.
- Bake for 12 to 14 minutes or until edges are light brown. Remove from oven and let cookies cool for 1 minute before transferring to cooling rack. (Yields 3 to 3½ dozen.)

www.cookbookresources.com

— —

Deluxe Oatmeal Cookies

⅓ cup (5⅓ tablespoons) butter, softened
1 egg
½ teaspoon vanilla

- Preheat oven to 350°. Empty contents of jar into large mixing bowl. Add butter, egg and vanilla.
- Beat on LOW speed until dough blends thoroughly.
- Roll heaping teaspoonful of dough into balls and place 3 inches apart on cookie baking sheet.
- Bake for 12 to 14 minutes or until edges are light brown. Remove from oven and let cookies cool for 1 minute before transferring to cooling rack. (Yields 3 to 3½ dozen.)

www.cookbookresources.com

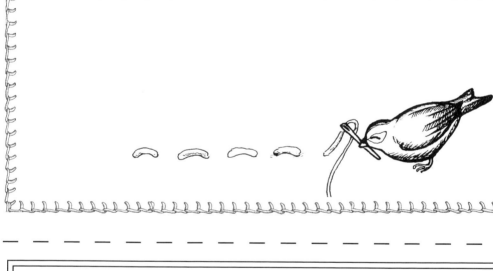

Mom's Chocolate Snickerdoodles

*This is a spin on an old favorite: chocolate-flavored
cookies coated with cinnamon and sugar.*

Ingredients for jar:

1⅓ cups sugar
¼ cup cocoa powder
1¾ cups flour
½ teaspoon baking powder
¾ cup finely chopped or ground pecans

Instructions for filling jar:

- Place sugar in 1-quart jar and smooth over.

- Gently spoon cocoa powder evenly over sugar.

- Spoon flour and baking powder over cocoa and press
  down lightly.

- Add pecans to jar on top of flour and press down firmly.
  Place lid on jar to close.

Continued next page...

*I am only one, but I am one. I cannot do
everything, but I can do something. And
because I cannot do everything, I will not
refuse to do something that I can do. What I can do,
I should do. And what I should do, by the grace of
God, I will do.*

-Edward Everett Hale

Continued from previous page...

Instructions for baking:

1 egg
¾ cup (1½ sticks) butter, softened
2 tablespoons milk
1 teaspoon vanilla
3 tablespoons sugar
1½ teaspoons cinnamon

* Preheat oven to 375°. Empty contents of jar into large mixing bowl. Add egg, butter, milk and vanilla. Beat on LOW speed or by hand until dough blends well. Cover dough and refrigerate for 1 hour.

* In small, bowl, combine 3 tablespoons sugar and 1½ teaspoons cinnamon. Stir and mix well. Roll dough pieces into 1-inch balls. Roll balls in sugar-cinnamon mixture and place 2 inches apart on cookie baking sheet.

* Bake for 10 to 11 minutes or until light brown around edges. Remove from oven, let cookies cool for 1 minute and transfer to cooling rack. Yields about 4 dozen.

President James Monroe said of the most respected ethics courses taught in colleges that "the question to be asked at the end of an educational step is not 'What has the student learned?' but 'What has the student become?'"

Mom's Chocolate Snickerdoodles

1 egg
¾ cup (1½ sticks) butter, softened
2 tablespoons milk
1 teaspoon vanilla
3 tablespoons sugar
1½ teaspoons cinnamon

- Preheat oven to 375°. Empty contents of jar into large mixing bowl. Add egg, butter, milk and vanilla. Beat on LOW speed or by hand until dough blends well. Cover dough and refrigerate for 1 hour.
- In small, bowl, combine 3 tablespoons sugar and 1½ teaspoons cinnamon. Stir and mix well. Roll dough pieces into 1-inch balls. Roll balls in sugar-cinnamon mixture and place 2 inches apart on cookie baking sheet.
- Bake for 10 to 11 minutes or until light brown around edges. Remove from oven, let cookies cool for 1 minute and transfer to cooling rack. Yields about 4 dozen.   www.cookbookresources.com

Mom's Chocolate Snickerdoodles

1 egg
¾ cup (1½ sticks) butter, softened
2 tablespoons milk
1 teaspoon vanilla
3 tablespoons sugar
1½ teaspoons cinnamon

- Preheat oven to 375°. Empty contents of jar into large mixing bowl. Add egg, butter, milk and vanilla. Beat on LOW speed or by hand until dough blends well. Cover dough and refrigerate for 1 hour.
- In small, bowl, combine 3 tablespoons sugar and 1½ teaspoons cinnamon. Stir and mix well. Roll dough pieces into 1-inch balls. Roll balls in sugar-cinnamon mixture and place 2 inches apart on cookie baking sheet.
- Bake for 10 to 11 minutes or until light brown around edges. Remove from oven, let cookies cool for 1 minute and transfer to cooling rack. Yields about 4 dozen.   www.cookbookresources.com

Mom's Chocolate Snickerdoodles

1 egg
¾ cup (1½ sticks) butter, softened
2 tablespoons milk
1 teaspoon vanilla
3 tablespoons sugar
1½ teaspoons cinnamon

- Preheat oven to 375°. Empty contents of jar into large mixing bowl. Add egg, butter, milk and vanilla. Beat on LOW speed or by hand until dough blends well. Cover dough and refrigerate for 1 hour.
- In small, bowl, combine 3 tablespoons sugar and 1½ teaspoons cinnamon. Stir and mix well. Roll dough pieces into 1-inch balls. Roll balls in sugar-cinnamon mixture and place 2 inches apart on cookie baking sheet.
- Bake for 10 to 11 minutes or until light brown around edges. Remove from oven, let cookies cool for 1 minute and transfer to cooling rack. Yields about 4 dozen.   www.cookbookresources.com

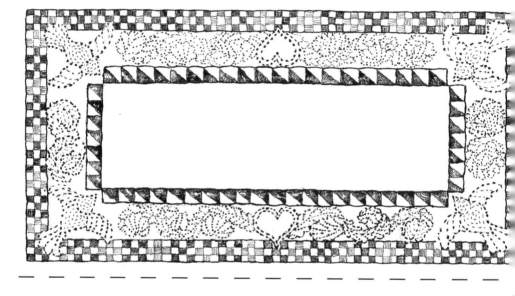

Orange-Sugar Cookies

These delicately-flavored sugar cookies have a hint of orange and distinctive flavor of almonds. They look so pretty in the jar with the alternating bands of orange. To make this an extra-special gift, attach a cookie cutter to the jar with a ribbon.

Ingredients for jar:

1 cup sugar
4 drops red food coloring
4 drops yellow food coloring
3 cups flour
3 tablespoons dried, ground orange peel*
1 teaspoon baking soda
2 teaspoons baking powder
½ cup finely ground almonds, toasted**

Instructions for filling jar:

- Place sugar in small bowl and add red and yellow food coloring. Stir well to color sugar evenly. (You'll end up with a nice orange color.)

- In medium bowl, combine flour, orange peel, baking soda and baking powder. Stir well to mix.

- Place half sugar mixture in 1-quart jar and smooth over. Spoon half flour mixture on top, press down and smooth over.

- Place remaining half sugar mixture over flour layer and press down evenly. Spoon remaining half flour mixture on top, press down and smooth over.

- Place toasted almonds on top of flour mixture and press down firmly. (It's a tight squeeze.)

- Place lid on jar.

TIP: Dried, ground orange peel can be found in spice section of your grocery store.

**TIP: To toast almonds and bring out flavor, place on baking sheet and bake at 350° for 5 minutes until light brown. Check frequently because they can burn quickly. Let them cool before adding to jar.*

Continued next page...

Continued from previous page...

Instructions for baking:

½ cup (1 stick) butter, softened
½ teaspoon vanilla extract
1 egg
½ cup milk

- Place contents of jar into large bowl. Add butter, vanilla extract, egg and milk.

- Beat on low speed to blend. For drop cookies, drop dough by rounded teaspoonfuls onto cookie baking sheet.

- For rolled cookies, refrigerate dough for 2 hours (to make it easier to work with). Roll out on lightly floured surface to ⅛" thick. Cut with cookie cutter and place cutouts on cookie baking sheet.

- Bake for 10 minutes. Remove cookies from oven, let cool for 1 minute and transfer to cooling rack. Yields 3½ to 4 dozen.

> *The best and most beautiful things in the world cannot be seen, or even touched. They must be felt with the heart.*
> *–Helen Keller*

Orange-Sugar Cookies

½ cup (1 stick) butter, softened
½ teaspoon vanilla
1 egg
½ cup milk

- Place contents of jar into large bowl. Add butter, vanilla, egg and milk.
- Beat on low speed to blend. For drop cookies, drop dough by rounded teaspoonful onto cookie baking sheet.
- For rolled cookies, refrigerate dough for 2 hours to make it easier to work with. Roll out on lightly floured surface to ⅛" thick. Cut with cookie cutter and place cutouts on cookie baking sheet.
- Bake for 10 minutes. Remove cookies from oven, let cool for 1 minute and transfer to cooling rack. Yields 3½ to 4 dozen.

www.cookbookresources.com

- -

Orange-Sugar Cookies

½ cup (1 stick) butter, softened
½ teaspoon vanilla
1 egg
½ cup milk

- Place contents of jar into large bowl. Add butter, vanilla, egg and milk.
- Beat on low speed to blend. For drop cookies, drop dough by rounded teaspoonful onto cookie baking sheet.
- For rolled cookies, refrigerate dough for 2 hours to make it easier to work with. Roll out on lightly floured surface to ⅛" thick. Cut with cookie cutter and place cutouts on cookie baking sheet.
- Bake for 10 minutes. Remove cookies from oven, let cool for 1 minute and transfer to cooling rack. Yields 3½ to 4 dozen.

www.cookbookresources.com

- -

Orange-Sugar Cookies

½ cup (1 stick) butter, softened
½ teaspoon vanilla
1 egg
½ cup milk

- Place contents of jar into large bowl. Add butter, vanilla, egg and milk.
- Beat on low speed to blend. For drop cookies, drop dough by rounded teaspoonful onto cookie baking sheet.
- For rolled cookies, refrigerate dough for 2 hours to make it easier to work with. Roll out on lightly floured surface to ⅛" thick. Cut with cookie cutter and place cutouts on cookie baking sheet.
- Bake for 10 minutes. Remove cookies from oven, let cool for 1 minute and transfer to cooling rack. Yields 3½ to 4 dozen.

www.cookbookresources.com

Basic Cookie Dough Solution

Be ready to bake homemade cookies anytime the kids bring friends over, a neighbor drops by or you're just hungry for some hot, homemade cookies. Keep this Basic Cookie Dough in the refrigerator or freezer and you're ready to go.

The recipes that follow use the Basic Cookie Dough to make 5 different cookies. You will love making cookies at a minute's notice and you will please all those who eat them.

Nutty Lemon Rounds
Traditional Chocolate Chip Cookies
Crispy Pecan Thins
White Chocolate Macadamia Nut Cookies
Peanut Butter-Jelly Thumbprints

Basic Cookie Dough

½ cup (1 stick) butter, softened
1 cup sugar
1 egg
½ teaspoon vanilla
1 teaspoon baking powder
2 cups flour

- In large bowl, cream butter and sugar. Add egg and vanilla and beat until light and fluffy.

- In medium bowl, sift ½ teaspoon salt, baking powder and flour together. Gradually add to butter mixture and beat well after each addition.

- Cover and refrigerate dough until ready to use. Warm to room temperature before using unless recipe specifies otherwise.

Nutty Lemon Rounds

1 recipe *Basic Cookie Dough (page 222)*
3 tablespoons lemon juice
2 teaspoons lemon zest (grated lemon rind)
½ cup coconut
½ cup finely chopped pecans
2 tablespoons sugar

- Preheat oven to 375°. In medium bowl, combine Basic Cookie Dough with lemon juice and lemon zest. Beat until ingredients mix well. Stir in coconut and pecans.

- Roll dough into balls about 1½-inches wide and place 2 inches apart on unsprayed baking sheet. Gently flatten with lightly-greased bottom of glass dipped in sugar.

- Bake 9 to 11 minutes or until edges begin to brown. Remove cookies from oven, let cool for 1 minute and transfer to cooling rack. Yields 4½ to 5 dozen.

10 Good Reasons to Have Meals at Home are included in this cookbook. Here's one of them.

10. Children who eat at home almost every night during the week are more likely to make better grades and perform better in school than those who do not. In 1994 in a Reader's Digest *national poll of high school seniors, Lou Harris reported higher school scores among seniors who ate with their families. He also found that these high school seniors were happier with themselves and their prospects for the future than seniors who did not eat at home regularly.*

Traditional Chocolate Chip Cookies

1 recipe *Basic Cookie Dough (page 222)*
½ cup shortening
½ cup packed brown sugar
½ teaspoon baking soda
1 egg white
2 cups semi-sweet chocolate chips
1 cup chopped pecans or walnuts

- Preheat oven to 375°. In large bowl, combine shortening, brown sugar, baking soda and egg white with Basic Cookie Dough. Beat until ingredients mix well. Stir in chocolate chips and nuts.

- Drop heaping teaspoonfuls on unsprayed baking sheet and bake for 10 to 12 minutes or until nicely brown all over.

- Remove cookies from oven, cool for 1 minute and transfer to cooling rack. Yields 4 to 4½ dozen.

Os Guinness wrote in his book Time for Truth *that in a "postmodern world, the question is no longer 'Is it true?' but rather 'Whose truth is it?' and 'Which power stands to gain?'"*

Crispy Pecan Thins

*These thin little cookies are crisp and crunchy.
If you like the taste of cinnamon, add ½ teaspoonful
to the dough along with the other ingredients.*

1 recipe *Basic Cookie Dough (page 222)*
½ cup shortening
¾ cup packed brown sugar
½ teaspoon baking soda
1 egg white
1½ cups coarsely chopped pecans

- Preheat oven to 375°. In large mixing bowl, combine shortening, brown sugar, baking soda and egg white with Basic Cookie Dough. Beat until ingredients mix well. Stir in pecans

- Drop by heaping teaspoonfuls on unsprayed baking sheet and bake for 12 to 14 minutes or until nicely brown all over.

- Remove cookies from oven, cool for 1 minute and transfer to cooling rack. Yields 4 to 4½ dozen.

 "Crazy Quilts" were usually lap or throw size and made purely as a decorating statement so no batting was needed. The fabric layers and thickness made it impossible to stitch and most were tied or simply tacked to the backing.

White Chocolate
Macadamia Nut Cookies

1 recipe *Basic Cookie Dough (page 222)*
½ cup shortening
½ cup packed brown sugar
½ teaspoon baking soda
1 egg white
2 cups white chocolate chips
1 cup coarsely chopped macadamia nuts, toasted

- Preheat oven to 375°. In large bowl, combine shortening, brown sugar, baking soda and egg white with Basic Cookie Dough. Beat until ingredients mix well. Stir in white chocolate chips and macadamia nuts.

- Drop by heaping teaspoonfuls on unsprayed baking sheet and bake for 10 to 12 minutes or until nicely brown all over.

- Remove cookies from oven, cool for 1 minute and transfer to cooling rack. Yields 4 to 4½ dozen.

Beware the young doctor and the old barber.
-Benjamin Franklin

Peanut Butter-Jelly Thumbprints

This cookie combines the age-old comfort food favorite, peanut butter and jelly, into a delicious cookie that can be made in a snap. Fast and easy!

1 recipe *Basic Cookie Dough (page 222)*
1 cup creamy peanut butter
½ cup packed brown sugar
3 tablespoons sugar
¼ cup grape jam or jelly

- Preheat oven to 375°. In large bowl, combine Basic Cookie Dough with peanut butter and brown sugar. Beat until all ingredients mix well. (Dough will be stiff.)

- Form dough into balls 1½-inch wide. Roll dough balls in sugar and place 2 inches apart on unsprayed baking sheet. Using back of blunt-handled spoon or your thumb, make indentation on top of each ball.

- Fill with about ½ teaspoon or less of jelly or jam.

- Bake for 8 to 10 minutes or until edges begin to brown. Remove from oven, cool for 1 minute and transfer to cooling rack. Yields 3½ to 4 dozen.

Textile companies incorporated metal into silk to add weight to the fabric and enhance the rustling effect of Victorian lady's gowns. However, the metals used in the silk fabric of the beautiful "Crazy Quilts" caused them to deteriorate.

Baylor Cookies

This is an old "ice box" cookie recipe that dates back to 1944 from the family who gave it to us. Shortening is not used much any more, but it works well in this recipe.

1 cup shortening
$\frac{1}{4}$ cup firmly packed brown sugar
1 cup sugar
1 egg
$1\frac{1}{2}$ teaspoons vanilla
$\frac{1}{3}$ teaspoon salt
2 cups flour
2 teaspoons baking powder
1 cup chopped nuts

- In bowl, combine shortening, sugars, egg and vanilla and mix until creamy. Add salt, flour and baking powder and mix thoroughly. Stir in nuts. Batter will be stiff. Refrigerate several hours.

- Divide batter into 2 batches and roll out to $\frac{1}{4}$-inch thickness on lightly floured wax paper. Dip edges of cookie cutter in sugar or flour and cut out favorite shapes. Bake at 350° for about 8 to 10 minutes or until light brown.

Quilting fell from favor in the early 1900's but roared back into popularity in the 1920's, 30's and 40's. Quilts are made with soft pastel colored fabrics. Applique patterns of pansies, irises and morning glories seemed to reflect the times.

Sweetheart Cookies

Super Easy!

1 (20 ounce) package refrigerated sugar cookie dough
1 (16 ounce) can white frosting
Red food coloring
Powdered sugar
Decorating stars, hearts and sprinkles

- Prepare dough. Lightly flour wax paper and roll out dough to $\frac{1}{4}$-inch thickness. Dip edges of heart-shaped cookie cutter in sugar and cut out as many hearts as possible.

- Place half heart cut outs on sprayed baking sheet. Cut out smaller hearts from remaining half hearts using a sharp knife. Separate from outside. Place smaller hearts on top of larger hearts on baking sheet.

- Bake at 350° for about 8 to 10 minutes. Use food coloring to tint frosting and spread on cookies. Decorate with stars, tiny hearts and sprinkles.

Success is a lousy teacher. It seduces smart people into thinking they can't lose.
-Bill Gates

Ginger Crinkles

1 cup (2 sticks) butter, softened
⅓ cup shortening
2 cups sugar
2 eggs
½ cup molasses
3 teaspoons baking soda
2 teaspoons cinnamon
½ teaspoon cloves
2 teaspoons ginger
4½ cups flour
Sugar
Powdered sugar

- Preheat oven at 350°. In mixing bowl, combine shortening butter, sugar, eggs and molasses and beat until smooth and creamy. Stir in baking soda, ½ teaspoon salt, cinnamon, cloves and ginger. Add flour and mix well.

- Shape cookies into 1-inch balls and refrigerate. Roll in sugar and bake for 12 minutes. Sprinkle powdered sugar over top of warm cookies with shaker or sift through strainer.

- To make gingerbread men, refrigerate dough and roll out on floured board. Cut with cookie cutter in shape of gingerbread man. Decorate or sprinkle with granulated sugar.

Why do I have to follow CNN on Twitter? If I want to follow CNN, I can follow them on CNN.
                              -Jon Stewart

Brownie Drop Cookies

1 (20 ounce) package fudge brownie mix
1 egg

- Combine brownie mix, egg and ¼ cup water in bowl and mix well. Dough will be stiff.

- Drop by teaspoonfuls onto lightly sprayed baking sheet and bake at 375° for 6 to 8 minutes.

- Cool slightly before removing from baking sheet.

Chocolate Chip Cookies

2 cups finely crushed graham cracker crumbs
1 cup chocolate chips
1 (14 ounce) can sweetened, condensed milk

- In bowl, combine all ingredients and mix well.

- Drop by teaspoonfuls onto sprayed cookie sheet and bake at 350° for 8 to 10 minutes.

You can't change the past, but you can ruin the present by worrying over the future.
-Anonymous

Oatmeal-Chocolate Chip Cookies

1 (18 ounce) box yellow cake mix
1 cup quick-cook rolled oats
¾ cup (1½ sticks) butter, softened
2 eggs
1 cup semi-sweet chocolate chips

- Preheat oven to 350°. In large bowl, combine cake mix, oats, butter and eggs and beat until they blend well. Stir in chocolate chips.

- Drop by teaspoonful on unsprayed baking sheet and bake for 10 to 12 minutes or until light brown.

- Allow cookies to cool slightly, remove from baking sheet and cool completely on wire rack.

Snappy Almond-Sugar Cookies

1 cup (2 sticks) butter
1 cup plus 2 tablespoons sugar, divided
½ teaspoon almond extract
2 cups flour
1 cup chopped almonds

- Preheat oven to 325°. With mixer, cream butter, 1 cup sugar and almond extract until light and fluffy. Slowly beat in flour and stir in nuts.

- Shape dough into roll, cover and refrigerate for 2 hours.

- Slice roll into ¼-inch pieces and bake for 20 minutes.

- Sprinkle with additional 2 tablespoons sugar while still hot.

Almond-Cranberry Crunchies

1 (17 ounce) box oatmeal-crisp cereal with almonds
1 (6 ounce) package sweetened, dried cranberries
1 (14 ounce) can sweetened, condensed milk
1 teaspoon almond extract

• Preheat oven to 325°. In large bowl, combine cereal, cranberries and condensed milk. Sprinkle with almond extract and toss to mix.

• Spoon into sprayed 9 x 13-inch baking pan and press mixture firmly with buttered fingers. Bake for 15 minutes, set aside to cool and cut into bars.

Peanut Butter Grahams

Great no-bake cookies.

½ cup light corn syrup
2 cups crunchy peanut butter
2 cups graham cracker crumbs
1 cup powdered sugar

• In large bowl, combine all ingredients and mix well.

• Shape into 1-inch balls and place on baking sheet lined with wax paper.

• Refrigerate for 30 minutes before serving.

An excellent health tip: Make Time to Pray.

Disappearing Cookies

1 (18 ounce) box butter cake mix
1 (3.4 ounce) package butterscotch instant pudding mix
1 cup oil
1 egg, beaten
1¼ cups chopped pecans

• In bowl, combine cake and pudding mixes and stir by hand, slowly adding oil.

• Add egg and mix thoroughly. Stir in pecans.

• With teaspoon, scoop cookie dough onto sprayed baking sheet about 2 inches apart.

• Bake at 350° for 8 or 9 minutes but do not overcook.

Cherry Macaroons

1 (14 ounce) can sweetened, condensed milk
1 (14 ounce) package shredded coconut
½ cup candied chopped cherries

• In bowl, combine all ingredients and mix well.

• Drop by teaspoonfuls on sprayed cookie sheets and bake at 350° for about 10 minutes or until light brown.

• Cool slightly and remove from pan.

TIP: Place extra cherry halves in middle of each macaroon before baking.

Peachy-Amaretto Crunch

2 (20 ounce) cans peach pie filling
½ cup amaretto liqueur
1 (18 ounce) white cake mix
1 cup slivered almonds, blanched
½ cup (1 stick) butter

- Preheat oven to 350°. Spread pie filling evenly in sprayed 9 x 13-inch baking dish.

- Pour amaretto over filling and sprinkle cake mix evenly over top of pie filling. Add slivered almonds.

- Slice butter into ⅛-inch slices and place over surface of cake mixture. Bake for 40 to 45 minutes or until top is brown.

Apricot Balls

Great no-bake sweets!

½ pound dried apricots, finely chopped
2 cups shredded coconut
½ (14 ounce) can sweetened, condensed milk

- In bowl, combine all ingredients and mix well. Refrigerate overnight.

- Shape into balls and set aside in covered container for 1 day before eating.

What did Snow White say when her photographs were ready? "I knew one day my prints would come."

Orange Balls

No baking for this recipe!

1 (12 ounce) box vanilla wafers, crushed
½ cup (1 stick) butter, melted
1 (16 ounce) box powdered sugar
1 (6 ounce) can frozen orange juice concentrate
1 cup finely chopped pecans

- In bowl, combine wafers, butter, sugar and orange juice and mix well.

- Form into balls and roll in chopped pecans. Store in airtight container.

TIP: Make these in finger shapes for something different. They make neat cookies for a party or for a tea.

Lemon Drops

½ (8 ounce) carton frozen whipped topping, thawed
1 (18 ounce) box lemon cake mix
1 egg
Powdered sugar

- In bowl, combine whipped topping and cake mix and stir by hand. Add egg to mixture and mix thoroughly.

- Shape into balls and roll in powdered sugar.

- Bake at 350° for 8 to 10 minutes but do not overcook.

Hello Dollies

1½ cups graham cracker crumbs
1 (6 ounce) package chocolate chips
1 cup coconut
1¼ cups chopped pecans
1 (14 ounce) can sweetened, condensed milk

• Sprinkle cracker crumbs in 9 x 9-inch baking pan. Layer chocolate chips, coconut and pecans.

• Pour condensed milk over top of layered ingredients. Bake at 350° for 25 to 30 minutes. Cool and cut into squares.

Nutty Orange Logs

No baking for these goodies!

1 (12 ounce) box vanilla wafers, crushed
½ cup (1 stick) butter, melted
1 (16 ounce) box powdered sugar
1 (6 ounce) can frozen orange juice, thawed, undiluted
1 cup finely chopped pecans

• In bowl, combine wafers, butter, sugar and orange juice and mix well.

• Form into balls and roll in chopped pecans.

• Store in airtight container.

My mother was the making of me. She was so true, so sure of me and I felt that I had someone to live for, someone I must not disappoint.
        –Thomas Edison

Rainbow Cookie Ribbons

White chocolate bits taste great in this too!

½ cup (1 stick) butter
2 cups graham cracker crumbs
1 (14 ounce) can sweetened, condensed milk
⅔ cup flaked coconut
1 cup chopped pecans
1 cup M&M's® plain chocolate candies

- In oven, melt butter in 9 x 13-inch baking pan.

- Sprinkle crumbs over butter and pour condensed milk over crumbs.

- Top with coconut, pecans and chocolate candies. Press down to even out.

- Bake at 350° for 25 to 30 minutes or until light brown.

- Cool and cut into bars.

White Chocolate Salties

8 (2 ounce) squares almond bark
1 cup packages salted Spanish peanuts
3 cups thin pretzel sticks, broken up

- Place almond bark in top of double boiler. Heat and stir until almond bark melts.

- Remove from heat and cool about 2 minutes. Add peanuts and pretzels; stir until coated.

- Drop by teaspoonfuls onto wax paper. Refrigerate for 20 minutes or until firm.

Chocolate Kisses

2 egg whites, room temperature
⅔ cup sugar
1 teaspoon vanilla
1¼ cups chopped pecans
1 (6 ounce) package chocolate chips

- Preheat oven to 375°. Beat egg whites until very stiff and blend in sugar, vanilla and dash of salt. Fold in pecans and chocolate chips.

- Drop on shiny side of foil on cookie sheet. Put cookies in oven, TURN OVEN OFF and leave overnight. If cookies are a little sticky, leave out in air to dry.

Easy Blonde Brownies

1 (1 pound) box light brown sugar
4 eggs
2 cups biscuit mix
2 cups chopped pecans

- Preheat oven to 350°. In mixing bowl, beat brown sugar, eggs and biscuit mix.

- Stir in pecans and pour into sprayed 9 x 13-inch baking dish.

- Bake for 35 minutes. Remove from oven, cool and cut into squares.

Let parents bequeath to their children not riches, but the spirit of reverence.
                                        –Plato

Corny Caramel Bars

Super no-bake bars.

5 - 6 cups caramel corn
1½ cups chopped walnuts
1 (10 ounce) package miniature marshmallows, divided
¼ cup (½ stick) butter
¾ cup butterscotch chips

- In large bowl, combine caramel corn, walnuts and half marshmallows.

- In heavy saucepan, melt butter. Add butterscotch chips and remaining marshmallows and cook over low heat. Stir constantly until mixture is smooth.

- Pour over caramel mixture and toss to coat. Press into sprayed 9 x 13-inch baking pan and press down with buttered hands.

- Cool before cutting into bars.

Butter Pecan Bars

1½ cups graham crackers, crushed
¼ cup (½ stick) butter, melted
1 (12 ounce) package butterscotch chips
1 cup chopped pecans
1 (12 ounce) jar caramel ice cream topping

- Preheat oven to 350°. In large bowl, combine crushed graham crackers and butter. Press into sprayed 9 x 13-inch baking dish and sprinkle with butterscotch chips and pecans.

- In microwave, heat caramel topping (lid removed) just until warm and thin enough to pour. Drizzle over top of bars and bake for 10 minutes or until chips melt. Cool and slice into bars.

Cashew Crunch

Great no-bake squares!

5 cups bite-size, crispy corn cereal squares
1¼ cups light corn syrup
1¼ cups sugar
1½ cups peanut butter
1 (9 ounce) can whole cashews

- Place cereal in sprayed 9 x 13-inch baking dish. In saucepan, combine corn syrup and sugar and boil for 1 minute.

- Remove from heat, stir in peanut butter and cashews and mix well.

- Pour mixture over cereal and cool. Cut into squares.

In the early 1920's, cotton prices were at their lowest. Feed and flour companies began to package products in fabric sacks. Women caught on to this and began using the fabric for sewing purposes.

As companies realized the trend, they became more competitive, and artists were hired to design fabric prints that would give their product an edge.

Sewing with "Feed Sack" or "Chicken Linen" was popular until the late 1940's. During World War II it was considered patriotic to use colorful sacks for clothing and quilting.

Apricot Cake

1 (18 ounce) box lemon cake mix
3 eggs, beaten slightly
1 (15 ounce) can apricots with juice, chopped

- In bowl, combine cake mix, eggs and apricots with juice and mix well.

- Bake in greased, floured 9 x 13-inch pan at 350° for 30 to 35 minutes or until cake tests done.

TIP: While cake is warm, you may frost with 1 cup apricot jam. Cool and cut into squares.

Cherry-Nut Cake

1 (18 ounce) box French vanilla cake mix
½ cup (1 stick) butter, melted
2 eggs
1 (20 ounce) can cherry pie filling
1 cup chopped pecans

- In large bowl, combine all ingredients and mix by hand.

- Pour into greased, floured bundt or tube pan.

- Bake at 350° for 1 hour. (Sprinkle powdered sugar on top of for a sweeter cake.)

An excellent health tip: Throw Away Something that You Haven't Used or Seen in the Past Year.

Coconut Cake Deluxe

This is a fabulous cake!

1 (18 ounce) box yellow cake mix
1 (14 ounce) can sweetened, condensed milk
1 (15 ounce) can coconut cream
1 (3 ounce) package flaked coconut
1 (8 ounce) carton frozen whipped topping, thawed

- In bowl, prepare cake mix according to package directions.
- Pour into greased, floured 9 x 13-inch baking pan and bake at 350° for 30 to 35 minutes or until toothpick inserted in center comes out clean.
- While cake is warm, punch holes in cake about 2 inches apart. Pour condensed milk over cake and spread around until all milk soaks into cake.
- Pour coconut cream over cake and sprinkle coconut on top.
- Cool, frost with whipped topping and refrigerate.

Quilters' Favorite Cake

1 (18 ounce) box yellow cake mix
3 eggs
1⅓ cup oil
1 (10 ounce) box dry coconut-pecan icing mix

- In mixing bowl, combine cake mix, eggs, 1¼ cups water and oil. Beat well.
- Stir in box of icing mix and pour into greased, floured bundt pan.
- Bake at 350° for 45 minutes. Test with toothpick.

TIP: *Some grocery stores do not carry this coconut-pecan icing, but the cake is worth looking for the icing. Keep these ingredients in your pantry so you'll have them whenever you want to take food to a friend.*

Fruit Cocktail Cake

1 (14 ounce) box yellow cake mix
3 eggs
1 (15 ounce) can fruit cocktail with liquid

• Combine all ingredients into large bowl and mix well.

• Pour into greased, floured 9 x 13-inch pan and bake at 350° for 45 to 50 minutes.

Old-Fashioned Applesauce Spice Cake

1 (18 ounce) box spice cake mix
3 eggs
1¼ cups applesauce
⅓ cup oil
1 cup chopped pecans

• Using mixer, combine cake mix, eggs, applesauce and oil. Beat at medium speed for 2 minutes. Stir in pecans.

• Pour into 9 x 13-inch greased, floured baking pan and bake at 350° for 40 minutes. Test until toothpick comes out clean. Cool.

• For frosting, use prepared vanilla frosting, adding ½ teaspoon cinnamon.

Super Oreo Cake

1 (18 ounce) box white cake mix
⅓ cup oil
4 egg whites
1¼ cups coarsely crushed Oreo® cookies

- Preheat oven to 350°. Grease and flour 2 (8 or 9-inch) round cake pans and set aside.

- In large mixing bowl, combine cake mix, 1¼ cups water, oil, and egg whites and blend on slow speed until moist.

- Beat 2 minutes on high speed and gently fold in coarsely crushed cookies.

- Pour batter into prepared pans and bake for 25 to 30 minutes or until toothpick inserted in center comes out clean.

- Cool for 10 minutes and remove from pan. Cool completely before frosting.

Frosting:

4¼ cups powdered sugar
1 cup (2 sticks) butter, softened
1 cup shortening
1 teaspoon almond flavoring
½ cup crushed Oreo® cookies
¾ cup chopped pecans

- With mixer, beat all ingredients except crushed cookie pieces.

- Spread frosting on first layer of cake and put second layer on top.

- Spread frosting over top layer and sprinkle crushed Oreo® cookies on top.

TIP: Sprinkle about ¾ cup chopped pecans over top of cake if you like.

Pound Cake Deluxe

1 bakery pound cake
1 (15 ounce) can crushed pineapple with juice
1 (3.4 ounce) package coconut instant pudding mix
1 (8 ounce) carton frozen whipped topping, thawed
½ cup flaked coconut

- Slice cake horizontally to make 3 layers.

- In bowl, mix pineapple, pudding and whipped topping and blend well.

- Spread mixture on each layer and sprinkle top of cake with coconut. Refrigerate.

Blueberry Pound Cake

1 (18 ounce) box yellow cake mix
1 (8 ounce) package cream cheese, softened
½ cup oil
4 eggs
1 (15 ounce) can whole blueberries, drained

- With mixer, combine all ingredients and beat for 3 minutes. Pour into greased, floured bundt or tube pan.

- Bake at 350° for 50 minutes. Test with toothpick to be sure cake is done.

- Sprinkle powdered sugar over top of cake.

Strawberry Pound Cake

1 (18 ounce) box strawberry cake mix
1 (3½ ounce) package instant pineapple pudding mix
⅓ cup oil
4 eggs
1 (3 ounce) package strawberry gelatin

• In mixing bowl, combine all ingredients plus 1 cup water and beat for 2 minutes at medium speed. Pour into greased, floured bundt pan.

• Bake at 325° for 55 to 60 minutes. Cake is done when toothpick comes out clean.

• Cool for 20 minutes before removing cake from pan. If you would like an icing, use commercial vanilla icing.

TIP: If you like coconut better than pineapple, use coconut cream pudding mix.

Easy Cheesecake

2 (8 ounce) packages cream cheese, softened
½ cup sugar
½ teaspoon vanilla
2 eggs
1 (9-inch) graham cracker piecrust

• In mixer, beat cream cheese, sugar, vanilla and eggs.

• Pour into piecrust and bake at 350° for 40 minutes. Cool.

• Serve with any pie filling.

Black Forest Pie

*This recipe is definitely a party dessert, but the family
will insist it should be served on a regular basis.*

4 (1 ounce) bars unsweetened baking chocolate
1 (14 ounce) can sweetened condensed milk
1 teaspoon almond extract
1 (20 ounce) can cherry pie filling, chilled
1½ cups whipping cream, whipped

* In saucepan over medium-low heat, melt chocolate with condensed milk and stir well to mix. Remove from heat and stir in extract.   (This mixture needs to cool.)

* When mixture is about room temperature, pour chocolate into whipped cream and fold gently until both mix well.

* Pour into prepared, cooked 9-inch piecrust.

* To serve, spoon cherry pie filling over each piece of pie.

Chocolate-Coconut Pie

1½ cups flaked coconut
1½ cups chopped pecans
1 (12 ounce) package chocolate chips
1 (6 ounce) prepared graham cracker piecrust
1 (14 ounce) can sweetened, condensed milk

* Preheat oven at 350°. In bowl, combine coconut, pecans and chocolate chips and mix well. Sprinkle mixture over piecrust.

* Spoon condensed milk evenly over coconut mixture and bake for 25 to 30 minutes.

* Cool before serving.

Creamy Lemon Pie

1 (8 ounce) package cream cheese, softened
1 (14 ounce) can sweetened, condensed milk
¼ cup lemon juice
1 (20 ounce) can lemon pie filling
1 (9 inch) graham cracker piecrust

- In mixing bowl, beat cream cheese until smooth. Add condensed milk and lemon juice and continue to beat until mixture is creamy.

- Fold in lemon pie filling and stir well.

- Pour into piecrust and refrigerate several hours. Slice before serving.

Creamy Pecan Pie

1½ cups light corn syrup
1 (3 ounce) package vanilla instant pudding
3 eggs
5⅓ tablespoons (⅔ stick) butter, melted
2 cups pecan halves
1 (9-inch deep dish) unbaked piecrust

- In bowl, combine corn syrup, pudding, eggs and butter and stir well. Fold in pecans. Pour mixture into piecrust. Cover piecrust edges with strips of foil to prevent excessive browning.

- Bake at 350° for 35 to 40 minutes or until center of pie is done.

Apple-Crumb Cobbler

2 cans apple slices
1¼ cup sugar
2 teaspoons lemon juice
¾ teaspoon cinnamon
1 (18 ounce) box white cake mix
½ cup (1 stick) butter, sliced

- Place apples in sprayed 9 x 13-inch baking pan. Sprinkle with sugar, lemon juice and cinnamon. Sprinkle cake mix over top and dot with butter.

- Bake at 350° for 40 minutes or until light brown.

Apricot Cobbler

So easy and so good!

1 (20 ounce) can apricot pie filling
1 (20 ounce) can crushed pineapple with juice
1 cup chopped pecans
1 (18 ounce) box yellow cake mix
1 cup (2 sticks) butter, melted

- Pour pie filling into sprayed 9 x 13-inch baking dish and spread evenly.

- Spoon pineapple with juice over pie filling. Sprinkle pecans over pineapple and sprinkle cake mix over pecans.

- Drizzle melted butter over cake mix and bake at 375° for 40 minutes or until light brown and crunchy.

- Serve hot or room temperature.

TIP: Top this cobbler recipe with whipped topping.

Blueberry Cobbler

½ cup (1 stick) butter, melted
1 cup self-rising flour
1¼ cups sugar
1 cup milk
1 (20 ounce) can blueberry pie filling
Frozen whipped topping, thawed

- Pour melted butter in 9-inch baking pan. In bowl, combine flour and sugar. Slowly add milk and stir. Pour flour-sugar mixture over melted butter, but do not stir.

- Spoon pie filling over batter and bake at 300° for 1 hour.

- Serve with whipped topping.

Cherry Cobbler

1 (20 ounce) can cherry pie filling
1 (18 ounce) box yellow or white cake mix
¾ cup (1½ sticks) butter, sliced

- Spread cherry pie filling in sprayed 9 x 13-inch baking dish and sprinkle with cake mix.

- Top with slices of butter and bake at 350° for about 35 minutes.

TIP: Substitute any other pie filling.

Choice Peach Crunch

2 (20 ounce) cans peach pie filling
1 (18 ounce) box white cake mix
1 cup slivered almonds
½ cup (1 stick) butter

- Preheat oven to 350°.

- Add pie filling evenly in sprayed, floured 9 x 13-inch baking pan.

- Sprinkle cake mix evenly and smooth over top. Sprinkle almonds evenly over cake mix.

- Slice butter into ⅛-inch slices and place over entire surface.

- Bake for 40 to 45 minutes or until top is brown.

The "Sunbonnet Sue" pattern with the distinctive little girl wearing a large bonnet first appeared in the late 1800's. A favorite since the 1920's and 1930's, it is also known as "Dutch Doll" and "Sun Bonnet Babies." The little bonnet girls were appliqued to muslin cloth and outlined with black embroidery floss. The pattern was often made as a "Charm Quilt" with each dress and bonnet made from different fabric.

Creamy Peanut Butter Fudge

3 cups sugar
¾ cup (1½ sticks) butter
⅔ cup evaporated milk
1 (10 ounce) package peanut butter-flavored morsels
1 (7 ounce) jar marshmallow creme

- In large saucepan, combine sugar, butter and evaporated milk. Bring to boil over medium heat and stir constantly.

- Cover and cook 3 minutes without stirring. Uncover and boil for 5 minutes (do not stir).

- Remove from heat, add morsels and stir until they melt. Stir in marshmallow creme and 1 teaspoon vanilla.

- Pour into sprayed 9 x 13-inch pan and place in freezer for 10 minutes.

Peanut Butter Fudge

1 cup milk
4 cups sugar
3 cups crunchy peanut butter
2 (7 ounce) jars marshmallow creme

- In large saucepan, combine milk and sugar and boil for 4½ minutes.

- Remove from heat and stir in peanut butter and marshmallow creme. Quickly pour into buttered 9 x 13-inch pan.

- Refrigerate and cut into squares.

Microwave Fudge

3 cups semi-sweet chocolate morsels
1 (14 ounce) can sweetened, condensed milk
¼ cup (½ stick) butter, cut into pieces
1 cup chopped walnuts

- Combine first 3 ingredients into 2-quart glass bowl. Microwave at MEDIUM 4 to 5 minutes and stir at 1½-minute intervals.

- Add walnuts and pour into sprayed 8-inch square dish. Refrigerate for 2 hours.

- Cut into squares.

Microwave Pralines

1½ cups packed brown sugar
⅔ cup half-and-half cream
2 tablespoons (¼ stick) butter, melted
1⅔ cups chopped pecans

- Combine brown sugar, half-and-half cream and a dash of salt in deep glass dish and mix well.

- Blend in butter and microwave on HIGH for 10 minutes. Stir once. Stir in pecans and cool for 1 minute.

- Beat by hand 4 to 5 minutes or until creamy and thick. The mixture will lose some of its gloss. Drop by tablespoonful onto wax paper.

Peanut Krispies

¾ cup (1½ sticks) butter
2 cups peanut butter
1 (16 ounce) box powdered sugar
3½ cups crispy rice cereal
¾ cup chopped peanuts

- In large saucepan, melt butter and add peanut butter. Mix well.

- Add powdered sugar, crispy rice cereal and peanuts to mixture and blend well.

- Drop by teaspoonfuls on wax paper.

Easy Holiday Mints

1 (16 ounce) package powdered sugar
3 tablespoons butter, softened
3½ tablespoons evaporated milk
¼ - ½ teaspoon peppermint or almond extract
Few drops desired food coloring

- Combine all ingredients in large mixing bowl and knead mixture until smooth.

- Shape mints in rubber candy molds and place on baking sheets.

- Cover with paper towel and let dry. Store in airtight container.

In the 1800's the first bakery was started on the yeast coast.

Brandied Fruit

Great gift idea!

2 (20 ounce) cans crushed pineapple
1 (16 ounce) can sliced peaches
2 (11 ounce) cans mandarin oranges
1 (10 ounce) jar maraschino cherries
1 cup brandy

- Let all fruit drain for 12 hours. For every cup of drained fruit, add ½ cup sugar.

- Let stand 12 hours. Add brandy, spoon into large jar and store in refrigerator.

- This mixture needs to set in refrigerator for 3 weeks.

TIP: Serve over ice cream, pound cake or angel food cake.

Simple Chocolate Fondue

1 (14 ounce) can sweetened, condensed milk
½ cup freshly brewed, strong coffee
4 - 5 squares semi-sweet baking chocolate, chopped
¼ cup peanut butter

- In saucepan, combine all ingredients and heat until mixture is creamy.

- Transfer to fondue pot and serve with chunks of pound cake, sugar cookies, apples or pretzels.

Angel Pudding Cake Squares

1 loaf angel food cake, cubed
1 (4 ounce) package chocolate pudding
1 (8 ounce) carton frozen whipped topping, thawed

- Place cake cubes in sprayed 9 x 13-inch pan or glass dish.

- Prepare pudding according to package directions and spread over cake cubes.

- Spread whipped topping over pudding and refrigerate for 6 hours.

- Cut into squares to serve.

Caramel-Amaretto Dessert

1 (9 ounce) bag small Heath® bars, crumbled
30 caramels
⅓ cup amaretto liqueur
½ cup sour cream
1 cup whipping cream

- Reserve about ⅓ cup crumbled Heath® bars (not in big chunks). In buttered 7 x 11-inch dish, spread candy crumbs.

- In saucepan, melt caramels with amaretto and cool to room temperature.

- Stir in creams and whip until thick. Pour into individual dessert dishes and top with reserved candy crumbs.

- Cover and freeze. Cut into squares to serve

TIP: *If desire, place crumbs in individual dessert glasses. Pour caramel cream over crumbs and sprinkle remaining crumbs on top. Wrap plastic over top and freeze.*

Divine Strawberries

This recipe creates a pretty bowl of fruit that's so delicious.

1 quart fresh strawberries
1 (20 ounce) can pineapple chunks, well-drained
2 bananas, sliced
1 (18 ounce) carton strawberry glaze

- Cut strawberries in half or in quarters if strawberries are very large.

- In bowl, combine cut strawberries with pineapple chunks and bananas.

- Fold in strawberry glaze and refrigerate.

TIP: This is wonderful served over pound cake or just by themselves in sherbet glasses.

Mango Cream

2 soft mangoes
½ gallon vanilla ice cream, softened
1 (6 ounce) can frozen lemonade, thawed
1 (8 ounce) carton frozen whipped topping, thawed

- Peel mangoes, cut slices around seeds and cut into small chunks.

- In large bowl, combine ice cream, lemonade and whipped topping. Mix well and fold in mango chunks.

- Quickly spoon mixture into parfait or sherbet glasses. Cover with plastic wrap and place in freezer.

Rocky's Dog Biscuits

*Don't leave your dog out when making cookies. Make these
great doggie treats with cookie cutter shapes he loves.*

1½ cups white or whole wheat flour
½ cup bran cereal
½ cup rolled oats
1 egg
½ cup low-fat milk
¼ cup oil
¼ cup chicken broth

- Combine flour, cereal and oats in bowl and mix well. In
  separate bowl, scramble egg with fork and stir in milk, oil and
  chicken broth. Pour liquid mixture into flour-cereal mixture
  and blend thoroughly.

- Lightly sprinkle flour on wax paper and roll out dough to
  ¼-inch thickness. Using cookie cutters, cut your dog's
  favorite shapes. Place on sprayed baking pan about 1 inch
  apart and bake at 350° for 10 to 12 minutes.

- Remove from oven, let "cookies" harden overnight or leave in
  oven overnight to make extra hard treats.

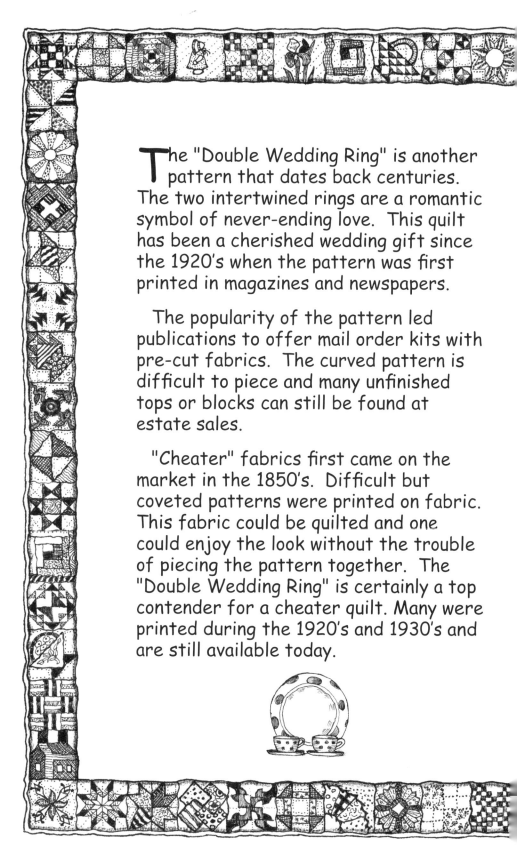

The "Double Wedding Ring" is another pattern that dates back centuries. The two intertwined rings are a romantic symbol of never-ending love. This quilt has been a cherished wedding gift since the 1920's when the pattern was first printed in magazines and newspapers.

The popularity of the pattern led publications to offer mail order kits with pre-cut fabrics. The curved pattern is difficult to piece and many unfinished tops or blocks can still be found at estate sales.

"Cheater" fabrics first came on the market in the 1850's. Difficult but coveted patterns were printed on fabric. This fabric could be quilted and one could enjoy the look without the trouble of piecing the pattern together. The "Double Wedding Ring" is certainly a top contender for a cheater quilt. Many were printed during the 1920's and 1930's and are still available today.

Easy Menus
for Everyday

You cannot help the poor by
destroying the rich. You cannot
strengthen the weak by weakening
the strong. You cannot bring about
prosperity by discouraging thrift. You
cannot lift the wage earner up by pulling
the wage payer down. You cannot
further the brotherhood of man by
inciting class hatred. You cannot build
character and courage by taking away
people's initiative and independence.
You cannot help people permanently by
doing for them, what they could and
should do for themselves.

-Abraham Lincoln

Each menu in this section has an entree and side dish. Serve as is or add a package of assorted greens for a salad and some bakery bread, if you like.

Menu: Sweet Honey-Fried Chicken
Tasty Baked Corn
Salad
Bread

Sweet Honey-Fried Chicken

1½ cups biscuit mix
½ teaspoon paprika
1 cup honey
4 - 6 boneless, skinless chicken breast halves

• Combine biscuit mix, paprika, mustard and a little salt and pepper in shallow bowl. Pour honey into separate shallow bowl.

• Coat chicken breast first in honey and then biscuit mixture. Heat about ¼-inch oil in heavy skillet and brown chicken on both sides.

• Reduce heat to low and cook uncovered for 15 minutes or until juices run clear. Serves 4 to 6.

Tasty Corn Bake

3 (15 ounce) cans whole kernel corn, drained
1 (10 ounce) can cream of corn soup
1 (16 ounce) jar salsa, divided
1 (8 ounce) package shredded Mexican 4-cheese blend, divided

• Preheat oven to 350°. Combine corn, corn soup, 1 cup salsa and 4 ounces cheese and mix well. Pour into sprayed 2-quart baking dish.

• Bake for 25 to 30 minutes or until bubbly on sides. Remove from oven and sprinkle remaining cheese on top. Heat another 3 or 4 minutes to melt cheese. Serve with remaining salsa. Serves 8 to 10.

When you don't have time to think, use these easy, timesaving menus for great meals.

Menu: Artichoke-Chicken Bake
Lemon Snap Peas
Salad
Bread

Artichoke-Chicken Bake

1 (14 ounce) jar artichoke hearts, drained, chopped
1 (8 ounce) package cubed Velveeta® cheese, divided
¾ cup mayonnaise
6 boneless, skinless chicken breast halves

- Preheat oven to 350°. In bowl, combine artichokes, ½ cheese and mayonnaise and mix well.

- Place chicken in sprayed 9 x 13-inch baking dish and spread artichoke mixture over each chicken breast.

- Bake uncovered for 40 minutes. Remove from oven, place remaining cheese cubes over chicken and cook another 10 minutes. Serve over hot, cooked rice. Serves 6.

Lemon Snap Peas

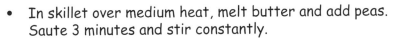

3 tablespoons butter
1 (16 ounce) package frozen snap peas, trimmed
1 teaspoon grated lemon zest
1 teaspoon fresh thyme

- In skillet over medium heat, melt butter and add peas. Saute 3 minutes and stir constantly.

- Add lemon zest and thyme. Cook an additional minute or until peas are tender-crisp. Serves 4 to 6.

Menu: **Peach-Glazed Chicken**
       Summer Spinach Salad
       Bread

Peach-Glazed Chicken

½ cup Italian salad dressing
1 teaspoon ground ginger
1 whole fryer chicken, quartered
½ cup peach preserves

- In shallow bowl, combine dressing and ginger and mix. Add chicken and turn to coat well. Cover and marinate in refrigerator 3 to 5 hours.

- Remove chicken, reserve ¼ cup marinade and boil 1 minute. Add preserves and stir until they melt. Broil chicken until it is no longer pink.

- Brush chicken with preserve mixture during last 5 minutes of cooking. Serves 4.

Summer Spinach Salad

1 (10 ounce) package fresh baby spinach
½ cantaloupe, peeled, cut into bite-size chunks
¾ cup red grapes, halved
½ cup coarsely chopped pecans, toasted
Poppy seed salad dressing

- Combine spinach, cantaloupe, grapes and pecans.

- Toss with poppy seed salad dressing. Serves 4.

TIP: Toast pecans in 275° oven for 10 minutes.

Menu: Baked Breaded Chicken
        Red Pepper Pasta
        Salad
        Bread

Baked Breaded Chicken

4 boneless, skinless chicken breast halves
½ cup mayonnaise
1¼ cups Italian-seasoned dry breadcrumbs

- Preheat oven to 375°.

- Brush both sides of chicken with mayonnaise and roll in crumbs until well coated. Place in sprayed baking pan and bake for 35 to 45 minutes or until there is no pink in chicken and juices runs clear when pierced with fork. Serves 4.

Red Pepper Pasta

2 (9 ounce) packages fresh spinach tortellini, cooked, drained
1 (7.25 ounce) jar roasted red peppers, rinsed, cut into strips
½ teaspoon dried basil
1 cup prepared ranch-style salad dressing

- In large saucepan, combine all ingredients and mix well.

- Cook over medium heat and stir several times. Serves 4 to 6.

My first desire for knowledge and my earliest passion for reading were awakened by my mother.
        -Charles Dickens

Menu: **Spicy Stuffed Chicken Breasts**
　　　 Potatoes au Gratin
　　　 Salad
　　　 Bread

Spicy Stuffed Chicken Breasts

4 ounces pepper jack cheese
4 boneless, skinless chicken breast halves
1 tablespoon taco seasoning
Oil

* Preheat oven to 350°. Cut cheese into 4 strips. Flatten chicken to ¼-inch thickness. Place strip of cheese down center of each chicken breast, fold chicken over cheese and secure with toothpicks. Rub each chicken roll with taco seasoning.

* In skillet with a little oil, brown chicken on all sides and place in sprayed 7 x 11-inch baking dish. Bake uncovered for 25 minutes or until juices run clear. Serves 4.

Potatoes au Gratin

1 (16 ounce) package frozen, shredded hash brown potatoes, thawed
1 (8 ounce) carton whipping cream
1 (8 ounce) package shredded cheddar-colby cheese, divided
4 fresh green onions, chopped

* Preheat oven to 350°. In large bowl, combine hash browns, whipping cream, half cheese, green onions plus generous amount of salt and pepper. Mix well.

* Transfer mixture to sprayed 7 x 11-inch baking dish. Bake 25 minutes or until hot and bubbly.

* Sprinkle remaining cheese on top and return to oven for another 5 minutes. Serves 6 to 8.

Menu: **Steak, Potatoes and Gravy**
Green Beans
Salad
Bread

Steak, Potatoes and Gravy

7 - 8 medium red, new potatoes, cut into 4 pieces
1½ pounds boneless beef sirloin steak, thinly sliced
1 onion, chopped
1 bell pepper, julienned
2 teaspoons minced garlic
⅓ cup cornstarch
1 (14 ounce) can beef broth

- In saucepan, cook potatoes in a little water over high heat for 10 to 15 minutes or until tender. Drain.
- In large skillet with a little oil, brown sirloin slices until beef is no longer pink. Place beef on platter and keep warm. In same skillet, saute onion, bell pepper and garlic using another tablespoon of oil.
- Return beef to skillet and add potatoes. Combine cornstarch and beef broth and pour into skillet. Bring mixture to boil, stir and cook for 2 minutes or until mixture is thick. Serves 6.

Green Beans

1 pound fresh green beans
2 tablespoons soy sauce
¼ teaspoon ground nutmeg
¼ cup (½ stick) butter
½ cup toasted sesame seeds

- Cook green beans in medium saucepan until tender-crisp, about 10 minutes.
- Combine soy sauce, nutmeg and butter in saucepan. Cook over medium heat for a few minutes. Add to green beans and toss lightly.
- Add sesame seeds and toss again. Serves 6.

Menu: Savory Herb Meatloaf
Mixed Vegetable Casserole
Salad
Bread

Savory Herb Meatloaf

1 pound ground round beef, browned
2 (10 ounce) cans cream of mushroom soup
1 (1 ounce) packet dry onion soup mix
1 cup cooked rice

- Preheat oven to 350°.

- Mix all ingredients in bowl. Place into sprayed 9 x 13 baking dish and form loaf.

- Bake for 50 minutes. Serves 4 to 6.

Mixed Vegetable Casserole

1 (16 ounce) package frozen mixed vegetables, thawed
1 (16 ounce) package frozen diced onions and bell peppers, thawed
1 (15 ounce) can Mexican stewed tomatoes
¼ cup (½ stick) butter, melted
3 tablespoons quick-cooking tapioca
1 (3 ounce) can French-fried onions

- Preheat oven to 350°. In large bowl, combine mixed vegetables, onions, bell peppers, and stewed tomatoes. Add 1 teaspoon salt, a little pepper and sugar and mix well. Stir in melted butter and tapioca.

- Transfer to sprayed 9 x 13-inch baking dish. Cover and bake for 45 minutes.

- Sprinkle fried onions over top of casserole and bake uncovered for another 15 minutes. Serves 8 to 10.

Menu: Pizza Dipping
Tossed Vegetable Salad

Pizza Dipping

1 large hamburger pizza, cooked
1 (26 ounce) jar chunky mushroom spaghetti sauce

- Cut pizza in half and then cut halves into 8 strips. Arrange on serving plate.

- In saucepan, heat spaghetti sauce and pour into round dish. Place dish in middle of serving plate with pizza strips. Serves 4.

TIP: To use this recipe for "supper", purchase a pizza you like best. There is also a large selection of different-flavored spaghetti sauces.!

Tossed Vegetable Salad

1 (10 ounce) package mixed spring salad greens
1 cup broccoli florets
1 cup sliced celery
1 red bell pepper, julienned
1 cup sliced zucchini
1 cup sliced baby carrots
Creamy ranch dressing

- In salad bowl, combine all ingredients except dressing.

- Toss with dressing. Serves 4.

TIP: Serve with bakery bread from the grocery store if you like.

I totally take back all those times I didn't want to take a nap when I was younger.

Menu: **Baked Onion-Mushroom Steak**
Cheddar Potato Bake
Salad
Bread

Baked Onion-Mushroom Steak

1¼ pounds (½ inch thick) round steak
1 (10 ounce) can cream of mushroom soup
1 (1 ounce) packet dry onion soup mix

• Preheat oven to 325°.

• Place steak in sprayed 9 x 13-inch baking dish and sprinkle with a little salt and pepper.

• Pour mushroom soup and ½ cup water over steak and sprinkle with onion soup mix.

• Cover and bake for 2 hours. Serves 8.

Continued next page...

I keep some people's phone number in my phone just so I know not to answer when they call.

Continued from previous page...

Cheddar Potato Bake

1 (7 ounce) box roasted garlic mashed potato mix
1 (8 ounce) carton sour cream
1½ cups shredded cheddar cheese, divided
1 (3 ounce) can cheddar French-fried onions

- Preheat oven to 375°. Prepare 2 potato pouches according to package directions. While hot, stir in sour cream and 1 cup cheese and mix well.

- Spoon into sprayed 2-quart baking dish and sprinkle with remaining cheese and fried onions.

- Bake 10 minutes or until casserole is hot and fried onions are golden. Serves 6.

The "Drunkard's Path" was created around 1849. The block is sometimes referred to as "Rocky Road to California" and "Country Husband." The squares used in this block can be rearranged in several different combinations to form new patterns. A few of the names include: "Wonder of the World", "Fool's Puzzle", "Vine of Friendship", "Falling Timbers", "Mill Wheel", "Indian Puzzle" and "Solomon's Puzzle."

The Drunkard's Path is closely associated with the Women's Christian Temperance Union founded in Ohio in 1874. Many quilts made with this pattern using the Suffrage movement's colors of blue and white reflected one's agreement with the cause or were sold in raffles or other fund-raising events to support the Union's activities. If you own an antique blue and white "Drunkard's Path" with WCTU penned or embroidered on it, you hold a part of history.

Menu: Delicious Pork Chops
20-Minute Linguine and Pesto
Salad
Bread

Delicious Pork Chops

¾ cup biscuit mix
1 teaspoon paprika
¾ cup Italian salad dressing
1 cup Italian breadcrumbs
4 pork chops
3 tablespoons vegetable oil

• Mix biscuit mix and paprika in shallow bowl. Pour dressing in second bowl and breadcrumbs in third bowl. Dip pork chops in biscuit mixture, in salad dressing and then breadcrumbs.

• In skillet, heat oil and cook pork chops for 5 to 8 minutes or until both sides brown lightly. Reduce heat to low, cover and cook for about 15 minutes longer. Drain on paper towels. Serves 4.

20-Minute Linguine and Pesto

1 (16 ounce) package linguine
¼ cup finely chopped parsley
¼ cup (½ stick) butter, melted
1 teaspoon fresh lemon zest

• In large saucepan, cook linguine according to package directions. Remove ⅔ cup pasta cooking liquid and set aside. Drain linguine but keep in saucepan.

Continued next page...

Continued from previous page...

Pesto Sauce:

⅓ cup extra virgin olive oil
3 teaspoons minced garlic
¼ teaspoon cayenne pepper

- In small saucepan, combine all pesto sauce ingredients and a little salt. Heat on medium heat until garlic is soft.

- Add Pesto Sauce to saucepan with linguine and stir. Fold in ⅔ cup pasta liquid, parsley, butter and lemon zest. Toss well. Serves 4 to 6.

TIP: Serve with packaged assorted greens and bakery bread from the grocery store if you like.

The 1976 Bicentennial revived the interest in quilting as once again women felt the need to commemorate a historical event. As in the past, this new generation of quilters connects to their personal lives, community and historical events with quilts. Their opinions and aid to causes are pieced and stitched into fabric works of art. Most importantly, they continue to give gifts of love and friendship.

Index

C

Q

R

S

Menus:

Page: 262
*Sweet Honey-Fried Chicken
Tasty Corn Bake
Salad
Bread*

Page: 263
*Artichoke-Chicken Bake
Lemon Snap Peas
Salad
Bread*

Page: 264
*Peach-Glazed Chicken
Summer Spinach Salad
Bread*

Page: 265
*Baked Breaded Chicken
Red Pepper Pasta
Salad
Bread*

Page: 266
*Spicy Stuffed Chicken Breasts
Potatoes au Gratin
Salad
Bread*

Page: 267
*Steak, Potatoes and Gravy
Green Beans
Salad
Bread*

Page: 268
*Savory Herb Meatloaf
Mixed Vegetable Casserole
Salad
Bread*

Page: 269
*Pizza Dipping
Tossed Vegetable Salad*

Page: 270
*Baked Onion-Mushroom Steak
Cheddar Potato Bake*

Page: 272
*Delicious Pork Chops
20-Minute Linguine and Pesto*

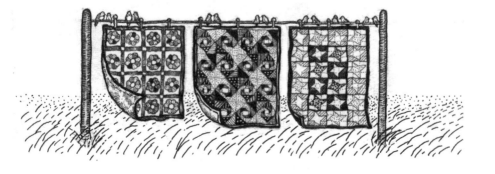

Cookbooks Published by Cookbook Resources, LLC
Bringing Family and Friends to the Table

The Best 1001 Short, Easy Recipes
1001 Slow Cooker Recipes
1001 Short, Easy, Inexpensive Recipes
1001 Fast Easy Recipes
1001 America's Favorite Recipes
Easy Slow Cooker Cookbook
Busy Woman's Slow Cooker Recipes
Busy Woman's Quick & Easy Recipes
365 Easy Soups and Stews
365 Easy Chicken Recipes
365 Easy One-Dish Recipes
365 Easy Soup Recipes
365 Easy Vegetarian Recipes
365 Easy Casserole Recipes
365 Easy Pasta Recipes
365 Easy Slow Cooker Recipes
Super Simple Cupcake Recipes
Leaving Home Cookbook
and Survival Guide
Essential 3-4-5 Ingredient Recipes
Ultimate 4 Ingredient Cookbook
Easy Cooking with 5 Ingredients
The Best of Cooking with 3 Ingredients
Easy Diabetic Recipes
Ultimate 4 Ingredient Diabetic Cookbook
4-Ingredient Recipes
for 30-Minute Meals
Cooking with Beer
The Washington Cookbook
The Pennsylvania Cookbook
The California Cookbook
Best-Loved New England Recipes
Best-Loved Canadian Recipes
Best-Loved Recipes
from the Pacific Northwest

Easy Slow Cooker Recipes
(Handbook with Photos)
Cool Smoothies (Handbook with Photos)
Easy Cupcake Recipes
(Handbook with Photos)
Easy Soup Recipes
(Handbook with Photos)
Classic Tex-Mex and Texas Cooking
Best-Loved Southern Recipes
Classic Southwest Cooking
Miss Sadie's Southern Cooking
Classic Pennsylvania Dutch Cooking
The Quilters' Cookbook
Healthy Cooking with 4 Ingredients
Trophy Hunters' Wild Game Cookbook
Recipe Keeper
Simple Old-Fashioned Baking
Quick Fixes with Cake Mixes
Kitchen Keepsakes
& More Kitchen Keepsakes
Cookbook 25 Years
Texas Longhorn Cookbook
Gifts for the Cookie Jar
All New Gifts for the Cookie Jar
The Big Bake Sale Cookbook
Easy One-Dish Meals
Easy Potluck Recipes
Easy Casseroles Cookbook
Easy Desserts
Sunday Night Suppers
Easy Church Suppers
365 Easy Meals
Gourmet Cooking with 5 Ingredients
Muffins In A Jar
A Little Taste of Texas
A Little Taste of Texas II
Ultimate Gifts for the Cookie Jar

cookbook resources LLC
www.cookbookresources.com
Toll-Free 866-229-2665
Your Ultimate Source for Easy Cookbooks